A *Thousand* LIVES

*Pithy Essays from Book Shops,
Coffee Pots and the COVID Crisis*

by

ANNABEL TOWNSEND

A Wood Dragon Book

OTHER BOOKS BY ANNABEL TOWNSEND

It Seemed Like A Good Idea At The Time:
10 years of misadventures in coffee
Pottersfield Press, 2018

Spilling the Beans:
The Concept of Quality in the Specialty Coffee Industry
Lambert Academic Press, 2012

A
Thousand
LIVES

Pithy Essays from Book Shops,
Coffee Pots and the COVID Crisis

by

ANNABEL TOWNSEND

A Wood Dragon Book

A THOUSAND LIVES:

Pithy Essays from Book Shops, Coffee Pots and the COVID Crisis
by Annabel Townsend

Cover art: Callum Jagger
Inside design: Christine Lee

Published by:
Wood Dragon Books
Post Office Box 429
Mossbank, Saskatchewan, Canada S0H3G0
www.wooddragonbooks.com

ISBN:
Paperback: 978-1990-863-356
Hardcover: 978-1990-863-400
eBook: 978-1990-863-394

Contact the author at: annabeltownsend.ca

DEDICATION

To Carl, Milo, and Theia—for their endless inspiration.

And to our furry critters who ate the first draft.

CONTENTS

1
CONVERSATIONS WITH FRIENDS

It was just another Monday afternoon in the pub, really; special only because my cousin Oliver was visiting from England. But otherwise, it was my friend Mackenzie and I, two pints of Belgian Moon beer, and a large plate of Irish Poutine (that is, "cheesy chips with stew on top" as my cousin referred to it). Oliver was staring at the food in confusion and sipping a local lager.

Nothing much was happening in the fall of 2019.

It seems like a lifetime ago.

Spending the odd afternoon in the pub is a habit that I have managed to keep from life in the UK, even though I am now in Saskatchewan, and the pub in question is an Irish bar in Regina. Mackenzie and I had been coming here for years, since our kids were tiny babies. We had met working for an insurance firm; I had left while I was pregnant to start an ill-fated coffee shop venture. Mackenzie had stayed and taken advantage of the generous year-long maternity leave offered by the company. Our daughters were born three days apart, and Mackenzie and I waved at each other across the labour ward of the hospital. Early on, we had enrolled our girls in the public library's story time program, mainly as an excuse to get ourselves out of the house and have adult conversations. Every week, we would bundle them up into strollers, exhaust them with stories and singalongs at the library, and then push the strollers filled with our sleepy infants to the pub and have a beer together while they napped.

Four years later, the girls are now in daycare, and my coffee shop is long gone. Mackenzie is on maternity leave again, Oliver had saved up enough money to come visit from England, and I was revelling in my newfound freedom. I had agonised over a recent decision to quit a job I had genuinely enjoyed, but which was badly paid and frustratingly inflexible. The baby that I had brought to the pub in a stroller for so long was now approaching kindergarten age, and I wanted more time with both of my kids while they were small enough to still be kids. I was brainstorming ideas for how to make a living doing something I enjoyed, that also allowed me time with my family.

This is all a euphemism for being unemployed. Yes, I was unemployed and sitting in a pub day-drinking with my friends.

Many things were discussed that day, although the favourite topic was the benefits to Oliver in moving to Saskatchewan. It would do him good, we thought. It would be nice to have him around. However, immigration is never as easy as that. There are annoyingly grounding things to worry about like moving costs, work permits, health coverage, and having somewhere to live, and Oliver is much more sensible and less impulsive than I am. Mackenzie could not, with any grain of plausibility, sell him on the idea of working at the insurance company, although she has definitely done well there herself. I did tell him he should take up the position I had just left—

but he reminded me that I'd left with good reason: the low wages.

It was at that point that they turned on me to ask what exactly I planned to do now that I was out of work again. Although I was comfortably settled in Canada, and had fought for and eventually achieved permanent residency status (meaning I was no longer reliant on the original employers that helped us emigrate), I still needed to work. Bills still needed to be paid, kids needed to be fed, and I knew I couldn't spend too long relishing in the freedom of afternoon pub sessions.

I did have the beginnings of an *idea*, however. I hadn't wanted to discuss this with the others yet, afraid as I was of their reactions. Friends can be the harshest critics, because being friends means that you value their opinions. Telling 'the world' on Twitter had been far easier.

I steeled myself to reply. If I couldn't tell my close friends and family with confidence, then what hope did I have?

"I want to open a bookstore," I said.

Their pause was unnerving. Then simultaneously, they said, "That's dumb. No one reads books anymore." (Oliver) and "Erm, I think there's probably a good reason why there aren't any other bookstores around here." (Mackenzie)

Sometimes, it's good to have these conversations with your nearest and dearest, so you know exactly whose opinions you should be ignoring.

2
THE BOOK MESS

"Why aren't you flying direct to Frankfurt?" she asked, one eyebrow arched in incredulity, red nails flicking through my pile of squashed paperwork.

It seemed a bit redundant to say, "Because it was $400 cheaper," since no one in their right mind would attempt this itinerary otherwise. Travelling from Toronto to Frankfurt via Lisbon, on a UK passport, post-Brexit, with a Canadian Permanent Residency card, a proof of vaccine certificate showing mixed doses, and during a pandemic is ... tricky. At least, convincing the woman at the airport check-in desk in Regina that this was a plausible journey proved tricky.

"It's your UK passport," she explained, tapping it. "It doesn't help."

She had no idea how fervently I agreed with her.

It was through reading *Around the World in Eighty Days* that I learned that the whole concept of passports and visas only came into being after World War I, when enforcing borders between nations became more strict. Although the character Phileas Fogg is fictional, it was not too much of a stretch for the author Jules Verne to suggest that if you looked determined enough in the late 19th century and were white and convincingly rich, you could go pretty much anywhere unquestioned. Nowadays, if you advocate for a "world without borders," you must be an anarchist. Armed with my "plague pass" (that is, my Covid-19 vaccine certificates from the Saskatchewan Health Authority), an Air Canada branded N95 mask, government-issued ID from two countries, and a Tim Horton's cup clutched reassuringly in one hand, I made it through check-in successfully, keeping my anarchic tendencies well-hidden for the time being.

I wasn't attempting to circumnavigate the globe in 80 days, but I did want to cross the Atlantic and part of the European Union, spend four days at the biggest book fair on the planet, and then come home again to Saskatchewan. In the pre-pandemic "before-times," flying internationally for a conference or business trip was still a privilege, but one that was more common and easier to accomplish.

Eventually, I made it through Toronto and across the Atlantic. My minor Covid-19 test-related panics in Portugal were resolved fairly speedily, despite my forgetting that with my British passport, I could no longer just breeze straight through immigration control in Lisbon, but had to wait in the much longer "non-EU" line. Yay Brexit. According to the airline's website, I needed to show *either* proof of double vaccination, or a negative Covid-19 test. However, at regular intervals in the line-up at Lisbon airport, there were signs in multiple languages telling us to have our vaccination certificates *and* negative test results ready for inspection. I had not done the PCR test, and was getting more and more worried the nearer I got to the passport control desk. Fortunately, the Portuguese border control staff seemed to have different instructions. The bored-looking man at the desk glanced at the words "Saskatchewan Health Authority" on my printed and crumpled piece of paper, then rifled through my passport for the photo page. He asked me to remove my mask for a second to see my face clearly

(I held my breath both for his safety and to quell my own anxiety) and then just waved me through. This was considerably less dramatic than I was expecting!

After nearly 14 hours of travel and now on a plane with dozens of other bookish types, I arrived in Frankfurt, Germany, and I was, indeed, a mess. My luggage, consisting of two changes of clothes, my emergency coffee supply and more than a dozen books, suddenly felt much heavier than it did when I left. After so long in Canada, I had also blissfully forgotten that rain is a thing that happens frequently in northern Europe, and I had not brought a jacket. I found a train heading out of the airport, and then my hostel room, and then sausage, spaetzle and a large beer—the necessities, of course—and collapsed into bed after wringing rain water out of my hair into the sink.

Frankfurt *Buchmesse* is such a huge event that it takes up an entire neighbourhood of the city, and fills six exhibition halls. Buchmesse means "book fair," but to my mind, it is as it is pronounced: "book-mess," and an enormous, multinational book mess sounds exactly like my sort of thing. It is the heart of the global publishing industry, with displays from the "Big Five" publishing houses down to the tiny presses releasing their first books. There were books in dozens of different languages, books in braille, picture books, art books, electronic kiosks with audiobooks and eBooks to download, pop-up books, textbooks, classics, journals, cookbooks, magazines, poetry books, books about other books …. Then there were seminars, workshops, author readings, and book launches. The whole place was populated with acquisitions teams and agents available to pitch to, freelance editors, publicists, copyright lawyers, cover designers, and of course, writers and artists from all over the world. It was a book lovers' paradise, and I lapped it all up.

After the event, I read that 77,000 people had attended the Buchmesse in 2021. This was an impossible, meaningless number to me. 77,000 is more than twice the entire population of Moose Jaw, Saskatchewan, and Moose Jaw is a *city*. It was more people than I had seen together in the whole of the last two years of the pandemic, and quite possibly the most people in one place that I've ever experienced in my life. Attendance at this Buchmesse was considerably lower than in previous years due to Covid-19, and it hadn't happened at all in 2020. I don't think I could have coped seeing it at full capacity!

I carried my bag of books around like a heavy, lumpy comfort blanket. Canada was the Guest Host of Honour at the Buchmesse that year (which is how I had scored cheaper entrance tickets) and there were several "big name" Canadian authors there. I had brought my copy of their books halfway round the world because I thought I had a better chance of meeting them in Frankfurt than I ever would have in Saskatchewan. (This may tell you more about Saskatchewan than Buchmesse.) I put some effort into dressing for the occasion in my red dress and uncomfortable high heels, then tracked down a few of these authors and fangirled embarrassingly at the Canada Night Gala where the keynote speech was given by Canada's brand-new Governor General, Mary Simon.

In the Canada Zone that took up an entire venue by itself, Margaret Atwood's disembodied head appeared on a screen, reciting some of her poetry over an art exhibit depicting the aurora borealis. There are certain moments in life where I find myself feeling as disembodied as that virtual Atwood head, and the Buchmesse was certainly one of them. The minute I had a chance to breathe and really appreciate my surroundings, I was overcome with incredulity that I was actually standing there, in Frankfurt, chasing bestselling authors and casually queuing up for coffee next to the

Head of Acquisitions from Penguin RandomHouse UK. How on earth had I ended up in this situation?

I was not attending Buchmesse as an author, nor did I have the confidence to try my luck with any of the agents or publishers there. Instead, I had justified the trip as a reconnaissance mission for my little bookstore in Regina, Saskatchewan. No indie bookstore owner *needs* to attend the Buchmesse, but I decided it definitely couldn't hurt to visit. The opportunity had presented itself, and so I leapt on it. It was my own personal "book mess" that had got me here—my own complicated narrative and some unique plot twists that had, somehow, led me to this surreal trade show. Not for the first time however, I felt like I was not fully in control of my own storyline. Truth is stranger than fiction, but my story certainly stretches the limits of the imagination for even the most devout fantasy reader.

On the flights out, I had been lucky. On the way back, I was not. After Buchmesse had concluded, I discovered my original flights: Frankfurt-Amsterdam-Calgary-Regina had been cancelled, and I was arbitrarily put on different ones—18 hours long with four separate hops that involved a two-hour layover in Edmonton without being able to leave the plane. I was exhausted after the event and I had to get back to work in my store. Also, I missed my kids terribly; it was one of only two times I had ever been away from them for more than a night. In a fit of frustration, I went down to the Frankfurt airport and argued and complained and nearly cried, until a sympathetic check-in desk worker took pity on me and scheduled me straight from Frankfurt to Vancouver. Having already checked out of my hostel, this left me with little choice but to wait out the next five hours until the Vancouver flight departed from Frankfurt airport. Giving me plenty of "alone" time with which to reflect on my journey.

I love the anonymity of airports. Specifically, airport bars. In most parts of the airport, the fellow passengers and grey featureless architecture form a monolithic and stressful assault on the senses. I know I am exceptionally lucky to have these travel opportunities, and I really shouldn't be complaining about cancelled flights and unidentifiable airline food and that jerk in front of me who puts his seat right back. In truth though, the luxury of air travel is often not very luxurious. But airport bars, during long layovers when travelling alone, are a special kind of seedy wonderfulness, and the part of the trip that I enjoy the most. The familiar, overpriced brand-name spirits, bottled then hung upside down, reflect the sick fluorescent lights present in every airport bar across the northern hemisphere. They do nothing but add to the placeless, timeless ambience. Acute lack of sleep, stress and excitement condense into a surreal transcendence; you are not Of This Place. No one is. But perhaps because of that, people are inclined to talk more. In a situation where you can genuinely be anyone from anywhere and no one can verify your claims, I find it odd that most people in those bars are disarmingly honest about themselves.

I arrived in Vancouver in the early evening although it didn't feel like evening after crossing so many time zones. Finding myself with several more hours to kill before I could get the connecting flight home to Regina, I had a watery, expensive beer, and started reading my book, *Station Eleven* by Emily St. John Mandel. The chapter I was reading was about a heroic airline captain deciding not to let his passengers deplane after the outbreak of a plague aboard, knowing he was condemning them all to death, but trying desperately to save everyone else in the airport. When the book was written ten years ago, it was still classed as fantasy; today it is more likely to be placed in a bookstore's current affairs section. Fortunately, I was interrupted at the really grim bit by someone trying to make conversation in the bar.

"What are you reading? Is it good?"

"Yep, very."

"Got a long wait?"

"Another few hours."

"Where are you headed?"

"Saskatchewan." (This one is usually a conversation killer.)

"Oh." (Long pause.) "You're travelling for work?"

"Well, I was. Off home now."

"So, what do you do?"

I silently dread that question, but I decided I was in a flippant mood. The best fantasy books, even dystopian ones, all require a degree of creative licence. In that vein dear reader, I invite you to suspend your disbelief when I say that I told him I am a real 'Doctor of Coffee'. It's true, I have a PhD from the University of Sheffield in the UK. I spent five years researching ideas of quality and waste in the specialty coffee industry before writing my thesis, which eventually became a book called *Spilling the Beans*.

This revelation generally makes it much easier to keep up a conversation. The follow up question is usually an incredulous, "What do you do with a PhD in coffee?" I have spent the last decade trying to answer that one, and I still don't have a coherent answer. And how I moved from coffee research in the UK to running an indie bookstore in Canada is far too complicated a tale for casual small talk in an airport bar.

I have never used my PhD for any academic or vocational purpose. In truth, having an obscure postgrad degree hinders your employment prospects in most circumstances. Certainly, teaching in academia is an option—but twelve years in the hallowed halls was enough for me. That epiphany came when I noticed one of my university supervisors had a sign on his door that read: *Please Do Not Mention The Outside World*. I knew I had to get out, if I were to maintain my tenuous grip on reality. Instead, I used my well-researched coffee trivia to open coffee shops, first in the UK, then after our emigration, in Canada too. These ventures took on many forms—from a vintage style tea room in Darlington in the grim northeast of England, to a coffee cart towed by bicycle at the Regina's Farmers' Market, and finally to my full cafe, Dr. Coffee's in downtown Regina that I reluctantly closed in 2017. Over the three years I owned Dr. Coffee's, it gradually became populated by writers and poets and we introduced a book exchange and hosted book groups there. My coffee adventures met with varying degrees of success, and all were extremely hard work. It took me several years to recover—financially as well as emotionally—before I was ready to try again. Dr. Coffee's Cafe was a coffee shop that had books in it. Now, I have a bookshop with coffee in it, and a year into the venture, I was still pretty confident that this was the way to go.

Strangely, I decided to skip over most of this when talking to that random traveler in the airport bar in Vancouver. For now, I am on an entirely new chapter, and there is far less coffee involved in this one. My pursuit of the perfect crop of coffee beans took me all over the world, and eventually led me to *books*. As I gave this man a potted history that concluded with my trip to the Buchmesse, the conversation dried up very quickly after he admitted he hadn't read a book since he was in high school.

George R.R. Martin, in the Game of Thrones volume *A Dance With Dragons*, points out the true value of reading. "A reader lives a thousand lives before he dies," he claims. "The man who never reads lives only one." I have taken this to heart. Next time I'm in another anonymous airport bar and drinking alone, maybe I shall invent another life. Hopefully, during the telling of my fictional life, my companion of the moment won't look at me like I have five heads.

I don't think I really want to live a thousand lives myself, fictional or otherwise. I'm quite content with the one I'm leading. I am not certain where this book-filled adventure began. But, as is evidenced by the Buchmesse, books touch many, many people. I think reaching out to a thousand other lives with a bookish venture somehow, is a plausible aim.

3

PEDAGOGY OF THE IMPRESSED

My bookish story started in Central America.

I had fallen in with the "wrong crowd" at university - as you do as an impressionable 20-something. This particular wrong crowd was the student branch of the Revolutionary Communist Party. I never had the patience nor political naivety to truly devote myself to all their causes, but at the time, I was heavily involved in the anti-war campaign as Tony Blair and George Bush decided to invade Iraq on very dubious grounds. My undergraduate degree was at the University of Durham in northeast England, an area full of old mining and steel towns that had never fully recovered from the demise of heavy industry and the closing of the coal pits in the 1980s. Outside the middle-class bubble of the university, unions and workers' rights groups still dominated the political landscape. Durham's anti-war protests were soon populated by the local Socialist Worker groups and in turn, the student communists. I made friends with a guy called Tom, who was and forever will be "Commie Tom" to me, even if he has mellowed somewhat in later life. Rather indirectly, Commie Tom introduced me to a few folks from the Nicaragua Solidarity Campaign. 2003 happened to be the 25th anniversary of the Nicaraguan Sandinista Revolution, and the group were trying to send a brigade out to Nicaragua to join the socialist festivities.

Needless to say, I really, really wanted to go, and suddenly developed a keen interest in Central American politics. Doubling as a fundraising effort, the official trip with the solidarity campaign was impossibly expensive. Even if I could have afforded it, I doubted that I had sufficient left-wing credentials to be eligible to officially be part of the trip. However, by then, the dream had taken root and so I decided to visit Nicaragua anyway, by myself.

I settled into Hospedaje Central, a backpackers' hostel in the middle of a town called Granada on the edge of the huge lake, Lago Nicaragua. A bed in the dorm room cost $2 a night, only marginally more expensive than a bottle of local beer at the bar. There were palm trees and yucca plants growing in the central courtyard, with hammocks strung up between them, colourful murals on the walls and small dark green geckos with yellow eyes crawling up the walls in the showers. It was a hippy backpacker paradise.

In this pre-internet, pre-smart phone era, my fellow hostellers were all journaling or sketching from those hammocks, with real pens on real paper. We used guide books to research that recommended hostel, and we got lost with paper maps trying to find it on the unnamed, unnumbered Nicaraguan streets. I had my *Lonely Planet Guide to Central America* (a weighty thing to cram into a backpack, ironically) and a Lonely Planet brand travel journal that became almost sacred to me. My journal had a waterproof cover and special pockets at the back for souvenirs like entrance tickets or trail maps or—those most rare of items now in 2022—properly printed photographs. None of the adventurers were writing blogs on laptops at the hostel; no one had any concept of "creating content" or photographing the hostel as an Instagram Influencer. If you wanted to type, you had to book some time in the nearby dial-up internet cafe.

As a consequence of this quaint, analog existence, quite a few of the hostel's inhabitants were in a constant search of something to read. Stupidly, the only reading material I'd thought to bring with me was *Pedagogy of the Oppressed* by Paulo Friere, which was half dissertation research, half Communist Party Imposter propaganda. I did plough through it eventually, learning about the socialist leanings of Latin American history, but it was certainly not the thing you could sprawl in a hammock to read while sipping fresh pineapple juice. Luckily, the hostel had curated quite an impressive library and book exchange and I raided it gleefully. One book really was the perfect hammock-read: a nonsense cosy mystery where a wronged hostess gains revenge on the guests who snubbed her at a dinner party by poisoning the guacamole. It contained recipes—essential reading for those rare occasions when I wanted to murder people for ordering avocado toast in my coffee shop.

Sometimes, I picked up the odd book left by another traveler. *Leaning Towards Infinity* by Sue Woolfe was something I would never have picked by myself; an Australian novel about three generations of women all of whom are very talented at abstract mathematics, the relationships between them and the problems of being female geniuses in a male-dominated academia. Like me, the book owner Johanna was British, a social science student, and travelling alone, "for the hell of it." Unlike me, she was not pretending to be a socialist revolutionary, and she had brought good books. She not only gave me *Leaning Towards Infinity*, but she wrote on the title page: *Dearest Belllllll. It was so good to meet, work and spend time with you. Good luck back in the UK - eat some Marmite on toast for me and enjoy the book,* ♥ *Johanna, August 2003.*

Despite her seemingly not knowing how many 'L's I have in my name, despite my loathing of marmite, and despite the novel having absolutely nothing to do with Nicaragua or our shared adventures, this dedication made the book special enough that I have kept it for nearly twenty years. Consequently, the book has now twice crossed the Atlantic. It came home to the UK with me in the early 2000s, and then moved to Canada with us in 2012. I find it extremely difficult to part with books at the best of times, let alone ones with mementos scrawled in them.

Although I returned to Nicaragua in 2008 to spend a year on coffee farms for my PhD, I still have my original Nicaraguan journal from 2003. The waterproof cover is coming off and the end pages are covered and stained with ground-in genuine Nicaraguan sand from the pacific beaches. In the front of the journal, I did my best to recreate one of the murals on the wall of Hospedaje Central: a beach scene with dramatic waves, a sunset and an inquisitive-looking exotic bird of some sort at the edge. In the centre, on the bright orange backdrop of the sunset on the mural wall, was inscribed a T.S. Eliot quote:

We shall not cease from exploration
And the end of all our exploring
Will be to arrive where we started
And know the place for the first time.

I have not read much T.S. Eliot, but that quotation struck a chord with me. I do not feel as though I've ceased my explorations, although I have, for the first time now, spent ten years in one Canadian city, Regina. Far removed from Granada, Nicaragua, and boasting well-marked roads and streets, Regina is a city I wish to fully explore, to really get to know.

My experiences in Nicaragua, while never directly leading to any career path, certainly had a profound influence on me. That trip was the first time I started to collect obscure books from obscure places, knowing even then that I would never be able to part with them easily. Lying in my hammock in Nicaragua, the thought never occurred that I would end up with my own store full of books, some 6500 km further north. My backpacking adventures slowed as the pressures of adulthood, family, work and a mortgage inevitably caught up with me, but the adventures contained in my books can still transport me across galaxies. As literature professor Mason Cooley once said, "Reading gives us somewhere to go when we have to stay where we are." These are dangerous words for a bookish entrepreneur to happen upon when faced with a global pandemic that restricted our travels for so long.

4
INSPIRATION FROM THE DA VINCI CODE

But maybe it *really* started with my book group.

It is a universally acknowledged truth that a man in possession of a "book exchange" must also be in possession of Dan Brown novels, several dog-eared John Grisham or Karen Slaughter paperbacks, and if you're really unlucky, a load of Harlequin romances.

In the book, *Good Omens*, by Terry Pratchett and Neil Gaiman, the character Crowley finds that every cassette he puts into his car's tape player magically turns into Queen's Greatest Hits. It is the same in book exchanges and Little Free Libraries the world over—all paperbacks, if they sit on the shelf long enough, eventually morph into books written by Dan Brown. During my coffee research travels, I found *The Da Vinci Code* in a youth hostel book exchange in Bloemfontein, South Africa, and *Angels and Demons* in a similar backpackers' place in Guatemala City. I started a book exchange in my coffee shop in Regina, and it took just three weeks for the first Dan Brown novel to be donated. Or grow there. Or for some other novel to mutate into it. When my neighbour's son kindly built us a Little Free Library outside my house in Regina, it only took four days to spot *Inferno*.

Back when no one had heard of Dan Brown, I attended a book group, with a friend aptly named Jane Storey. The book group was my solace: in the mid-2000s, I was a hard-up student, then completing my masters of arts studies, and woefully underemployed working in a chain coffee shop called Caffe Nero. I was not enjoying my MA: it was intensely theoretical and dry, there were far too many statistics involved and I did not know what I would do with the degree once I had completed it. I had reached the limit of my tolerance for the deprived and anti-social surroundings of Darlington, and my job was tiring, tedious, and entirely unfulfilling. I had no reasonable excuses to go travelling any more, but I also lacked the means to start my own business venture. In hindsight, I was also desperately lonely. I felt completely stuck and did not know what to do to remedy the situation. That was, until Jane invited me to the book group.

The Darlington Caffe Nero was distinguishable from every other Caffe Nero in the country only because it was lodged above the only bookshop in town, a branch of the British Waterstones chain. Unfortunately, Waterstones' hosting of the book group meant that our choice of books was limited to whatever the company head office wanted to promote each month. The organisers took the initiative to provide copious amounts of cheap red wine to fuel the discussions and soften the blow of having to read whatever recommendations came down from on high.

Then, we were given *The Da Vinci Code*.

Jane **hated** *The Da Vinci Code*. It wasn't that she was just disinterested, she possessed a loathing so pure it was almost tangible. Jane had paid for her copy of the book from Waterstones, and so she forced herself to meticulously read every single page before tearing out each piece of paper as she finished it, scrunching them into impossibly tiny, tight balls of rage and hurling them across her room. At the next meeting, Jane poured herself a giant glass of wine, gulped it down in one go and then brought out the little balls of paper from her purse. She'd brought all of them along to show us how much she'd hated the book, in case we hadn't got the message.

But why did Dan Brown inspire such vitriol? It wasn't because he "borrowed' quite a lot of the plot of *The Da Vinci Code* from a 1983 novel called *Holy Blood, Holy Grail*, without crediting its authors (and was then sued over it). It was not because of the predictability of the character arc. It wasn't even bitterness at Dan Brown's obvious success despite the seeming lack of editing in some of the later books. For example, the following excerpt is from his 2017 book, *Origin*:

"Robert," Ambra whispered, "just remember the wise words of Disney's Princess Elsa."

Langdon turned. "I'm sorry?"

Ambra smiled softly. "Let it go."

No, Jane's Dan Brown aversion was solely because of his writing style. "I hated it from the first sentence," she said. "It sounds like an obituary. And it never gets any better."

The opening line of *The Da Vinci Code* **does** sound like an obituary: *Renowned curator Jacques Saunière staggered through the vaulted archway of the museum's Grand Gallery.*

It's possible that the opening line sounds like an obituary because it is—Jacques Sauniere dies in the next three hundred words. But it reads weirdly for a novel, and to Jane and I, it sounded clunky and contrived. This obituary inclination gets weirder still, however, when you look at the opening lines of Brown's other novels: *Physicist Leonardo Vetra smelled burning flesh, and he knew it was his own. (Angels and Demons)* and *Geologist Charles Brophy had endured the savage splendor of this terrain for years, and yet nothing could prepare him for a fate as barbarous and unnatural as the one about to befall him. (Deception Point)*

As I am not a linguist, I looked this up to see why this formula is so irksome. Geoff Pullum at the University of Edinburgh helpfully explains in his Language Log blog that this is an "anarthrous occupational nominal premodifier," or in other words, a name following a disjointed description of a job. "Anarthrous" can also mean "having no legs," however, which admittedly makes it more relevant to the fate of Dan Brown's poor characters as they get chopped up and mutilated later on.

I do not hate Dan Brown novels as much as my friend Jane does, but I have never been motivated to stock them in my shop. Clearly, they are so ubiquitous in libraries, book exchanges, and used books stores that no one has ever asked for new editions in my store.

However, regardless of the quality of the writing, there was one line in *The Da Vinci Code* that did stick with me. It was Langdon yelling, "Quick! Get me to the library!" It's a blatant nod towards the well-known quote from Einstein: *The only thing that you absolutely have to know is the location of the library.* In my opinion, the line is so awful it's almost funny, yet it does convey the eternal importance of books, both in the mind of Brown and of his imaginary friend, Langdon. Even in the later novels, no one dares suggest to dear Langdon that he should "just Google it"—although if Brown took the characters down an internet rabbit-hole of conspiracy theories concerning the lives of important religious figures, the novels would have turned out very differently indeed. The author acknowledges the unspoken assumption in his writing that books contain truth, and have a gravitas that is not bestowed upon websites.

Books required for my studies offered truths and knowledge, but the books chosen for the book group provided entertainment and comfort and a welcome distraction when I was at my most miserable. Books allowed me to metaphorically leave Darlington. Books were an escape. I made friends in an unlikely place, through sharing books and wine. If I learned anything from *The Da Vinci Code*, it is that books are important, and Dan Brown *gets* it. For this reason alone, I tolerated his book long enough to witness Jane's amazing reaction to it, and I am richer for this experience.

5
COFFEE GEOGRAPHIES

It all started in Sheffield, really.

"We are reading the paper. It is Sunday and we are curious about our world."

Actually, it was a Tuesday afternoon, it was raining and at that moment I didn't care about the outside world, but this closing line of the preface to the wonderful book, *Glass, Paper, Beans* by Leah Hager Cohen had caught me up. She was describing a typical scene in her favourite café; almost dreamlike and nostalgic. Calm and very human somehow. I like the sound of the place after just three pages.

This book was given to me by Nissa, who works in the geography department of the University of Sheffield. Nissa is the sort of person others would describe as "bubbly." I prefer to think of her as "sunny"—she is so cheerful and smiling that she lit up our stress-filled postgrad office. I don't know her well, but it is such a rarity to be given a book by a vague acquaintance that I have eternally linked her to the author of *Glass, Paper,*

Beans. In my mind at least, she is the one sitting in that cafe, watching other people read the paper.

Idly, I wondered if anyone would ever describe an afternoon sitting in my cafe so beautifully. My coffee business didn't yet exist, but even so, I doubted it would ever have such a calming atmosphere.

Instead, I was sitting in someone else's cafe: Gusto Italiano, a coffee shop down the hill from my university in Sheffield, UK. I was waiting for my friend, Anna. As per usual, she was late, but Gusto Italiano is the sort of place where one can lounge around for hours, staring at the very pretty lattes. I bought one in anticipation, hoping she would arrive before the heart, skilfully drawn in the milk foam on top, sunk and dissolved into the espresso.

I am sceptical of places that advertise "genuine Italian coffee"—Italy is a long way away, after all—but this place won me over. It was a bit pricey for a student such as myself, but I was paying for the ambience, the Italian-ness, and the perceived sophistication—as well as the coffee. And avoiding our peers was a definite attraction at times too: it is nice to *not* be surrounded by other students constantly, as we would be at the coffee shop on campus.

The caffeine in my drink attached to adenosine receptors in my brain, blocking my natural fatigue from a late-night study session, sharpening my thought processes, and focusing my mind. I imagine coffee connections snaking out across my imaginary globe, linking up like synapses. I am British, sitting in an Italian-style coffee shop, waiting for my Polish crush, drinking coffee made on an imported Italian espresso machine from beans roasted in a German-designed roaster. At a now-educated guess, the beans were imported from a Central American cooperative or one of the huge plantations in Brazil through a brokerage in Seattle or maybe Amsterdam before being blended by experts at the roasting company—I squint at the packet of beans on the counter—on the Isle of Dogs in London. So many countries, so many characters, so many stories, all percolated into my hot and fragrant cup.

Anna really likes Gusto Italiano. The first time we came here, she immediately adopted the manager and jabbered away in fluent Italian about the merits of Italian wine. I remember thinking, *Where did she learn Italian?* We had talked about how we both ended up in Sheffield, the city of the steel industry, and now, Geography Post-graduate students too. I thought that she, being a polylingual PhD student from Poland, aged just 23, would have a far more interesting backstory than my own rather accidental journeys. I described my haphazard adventures from Kent in the southeast of England to a year in Peru, getting married to a guy from South Africa who I met on a bus in Wales, to moving "up north" once more to County Durham, to working in coffee shops to fund my academic habits, and finally winding up doing a doctorate degree about the coffee industry alongside her in this grey Yorkshire city. Anna looked at me, open-mouthed. "You've lived so many lives already!" she squeaked.

Sitting across from me that day in Gusto Italiano, she poked me affectionately with her umbrella, giggled and invited me to help devour a huge chunk of genuine Italian chocolate cake. Italian chocolate cake. Chocolate does not grow in Italy either, nor England. Anna licked chocolate ganache off her finger. I started to wonder about the story behind cocoa beans and the coffee cup gradually grew cold in my hands.

I admit it, I miss university. It was a wonderful luxury, being at liberty to read all day about things that interested me, without the pressures of producing anything commercially viable with my new-found knowledge. At one point, I believed I could quite happily moulder unspecifically in academia forever, if it wasn't for that pesky thing called "earning a living." My solution was, eventually, to open my own bookstore-cafe. The coffee shops came first, but literature has always pushed its way in, in some form.

These early entrepreneurial fantasies, along with genuine interest and the need to pad out my background chapter on coffee history for my thesis, led me to reading about the 17th-century coffee shops in Britain—which I found fascinating. Coffee first reached London around 1650 and became extremely popular, with coffee houses offering an alternative to taverns. Most were laid out with a coffee bar at one end and long benches to sit at, forcing strangers to sit next to each other. Unsurprisingly, this led to a breaking down of rank and social hierarchy if only within the coffee house, and people, well, men, began "free and open debates"—or in other words, plenty of informed, caffeinated arguing.

Many now-famous institutions have coffee shop origins, such as Lloyds of London that started out as a coffee shop where merchants met to conduct trades. Coffee houses in different places had particular themes— the ones around the theatres attracted the "wits" and critics and poets, the coffee shops near the printers were filled with pamphleteers, the former-day tabloid media, and the ones near the schools were filled with young scientists. "The Chemical Club," a precursor to The Royal Society, was originally founded by three men in a coffee shop in Oxford.

Markman Ellis, in his book, *The Coffee-House: A Cultural History* describes the power of attending a coffee house. *In the coffee houses men of science, learning and scholarship found they had unprecedented access to all kinds of knowledge: commercial, literary, mechanical, theological. Unlike the narrow confines of the schools, whether university, church or club, the coffee house opened the whole world of learning to the clientele. To a seventeenth century mind, entering a coffee house was like walking into the internet.*

And so, the Penny University was born: a place where you could receive a university education by listening to the other customers, all for the price of a cup of coffee. As well as being referred to by coffee fans as "penny universities" or "the free school of ingenuity," coffee shops were also called by their critics "a poseur's paradise." Nothing changes. Many people today—myself included—sit in coffee shops for hours, now equipped with laptops but still attempting to look intellectual. We just use social media to rant on rather than striking up a conversation with anyone else in the room, a disconnection from the past which I find quite tragic.

These coffee houses operated long before espresso machines and even before anyone thought to filter the coffee. The coffee in 1670's London was Turkish style, roasted in a pan over a fire, ground up roughly then boiled in water. Boiling the drink in this fashion certainly improved its safety, and lifted men out of the malaise of mild but perpetual drunkenness that came from a lifetime of drinking weak beer instead of contaminated water, but it often produced a drink that looked, smelled, and tasted like soot.

The customers of the coffee houses were exclusively men. Women could serve in the coffee houses, but could not be part of the conversations and therefore were not privy to the cheap education on offer there. Despite this, the idea of the Penny Universities speaks to me. Although I will do without the public autopsies on the coffee bar conducted by science students and the burnt beans and the exclusion of women, I will keep the caffeinated discourse, social space and pursuit of knowledge and creativity. I've come a long way, physically and emotionally from Gusto Italiano in Sheffield, but I still keep returning to the thought that coffee and books are a mighty combination. And what better name for a bookstore-cafe run by someone with a PhD in coffee?

6
WAYFINDING IN FLATLAND

I think it all began when we emigrated.

Moving to a different country is not a decision to make lightly, but eventually it was an easy decision for us to make. The UK in general, and the town of Darlington specifically, had not been kind to Carl and I. A combination of unfulfilling jobs, low pay, few friends, and no sense of community in the area—whilst feeling as though we were powerless to change these things—made for a miserable existence. We were both thoroughly sick of everything and constantly hunting for an escape. This feeling was made more acute when Milo was born, as we really did not want our children growing up in that area. When an opportunity presented itself to move to Canada, we knew that we had to make the leap or regret it forever.

Preparing to emigrate is a mammoth task. Carl and I began a period of manic clearing and packing. We are not exactly the minimalist type and so having to pack up our entire house— and the toddler and the pets—was a fresh form of torture for both of us. I'm sorry to report that it was neither *magical* nor *life-changing* on its own. None of it brought us joy directly; the consolation was solely the thought of escaping Darlington.

I bought a Kindle. One of the earliest models, long before touchscreens or colour graphics, where I had to press a button on the side to turn the page. I was not a fan of eBooks then and even less of one now. I just cannot concentrate on a screen for long enough to read a novel and so do not enjoy the process. At that point, fresh out of university, I still associated screens with work or studying and couldn't bring myself to turn one on merely for pleasure. Thirdly, I don't want to risk dropping the Kindle in the bath, which is the place I usually read novels, and is why a lot of my favourite books have curly edges to their pages.

But Kindles and e-readers do have the huge advantage that they can store an inordinate number of books, in very little space. Perfect for a transatlantic voyage, I thought! I looked for the digital versions of a few of my most beloved books, and discovered that most of them were still full price as eBooks. If I wanted to replace my entire book collection in Kindle format, it would have cost me thousands. In the end, I downloaded some classics that were 99 pence—or free if they were out of copyright—and kept the rest of my books as hardcopies. Nine crates of books went into the big blue shipping container, but still, I felt bereft of the ones I had to leave behind.

Preparing for emigration is not just about packing, however. It also involves learning about where we were going. That was also exceedingly difficult to do remotely. We had Skype and Google Earth to help visualise our new home from afar, and I befriended people on social media if they happened to have "Regina" or "YQR" (the airport code) in their profiles. Most of them told me not to look for places to live in North Central, but failed to explain why. I soon realised that if I wanted to get acclimatised culturally to Saskatchewan, I would have to look beyond social media.

There were only two TV shows available on BBC that I knew were authentically Canadian. *Aaargh, it's the Mr Hell Show!* was a late-night animation that featured an angry, violent seal cub called Serge, who used copious French-Canadian swear words and wanted to reap revenge on the fashion industry for killing his parents. The other was *Due South* starring Paul Gross as Benton Fraser, a naive Mountie who somehow wound up being a detective in Chicago while still wearing his red RCMP uniform. This show took on special significance to me, when I remembered one line in it: Benton Fraser is asked what was the largest city he had ever worked in. He replies, "Moose Jaw." A Saskatchewan connection! Woohoo!

With my sense of the Canadian people still reduced to stereotypes from British and American television, I turned again to books. I knew I should probably read Alice Munro, but I confess I got bored after just two of her dry, short stories. Atwood still reminds me of a module I took on feminist literature in high school, so I didn't fancy revisiting her either. I did discover Will Ferguson, who has written a great deal about the Canadian character—and I devoured *How to Be Canadian* as a textbook, and *Beauty Tips from Moose Jaw*. Ferguson is definitely not a fan of Saskatchewan, however, which was a little worrying at the time.

Despite the immense stress of the move, we finally made it to Canada. Milo and I arrived in Saskatchewan in April 2012. Carl followed in August, and our belongings finally joined us in early November. As soon as I arrived in Regina, I joined the library and started exploring the local CanLit. Without a TV and with a patchy internet connection borrowed from the restaurant below my tiny apartment, I found myself reading more than I had in years. I even ploughed through a biography of Stephen Harper. I had to renew it from the library three times as it was so heavy-going!

Saskatchewan's climate, politics, and culture is a sharp contrast both from the oppressive humidity and passionate, ideological Latinos that I encountered in Central America, and the damp, miserable greyness of the landscape and reserved, dry-humoured people in Northern England, but the cultural differences remain very difficult to articulate clearly. Eventually, I did find many fiction books set vaguely in "the prairies"—and many are grim stories of the Great Depression. (*Etta and Otto and Russell and James* by Emma Hooper springs to mind as the perfect example of bleak, prairie historical fiction.) Depression-era Saskatchewan was a fertile setting, if only for novelists and this style of literature felt distinctly 'Canadian' to me as a newcomer.

One historical prairie book that I devoured was *Dustship Glory* by Andreas Schroeder. Just outside of the city of Moose Jaw, a few thousand kilometres from the nearest ocean, is large ship known as the Sontianan. It was built by hand in the 1930s by a Finnish immigrant named Tom Sukanen. *Dustship Glory* is the fictionalised—but no less tragic—tale of how the ship came to be in the middle of the prairie and Sukanen's epic but sad adventures as he tried to escape the drought, poverty, and isolation of his environment. There is now a Sukanen ship museum explaining the incredible story, which, much like the Sandinista revolutionaries a decade before, was something fascinating that I never expected to discover on my travels.

As for Regina itself, I have come across very few fiction books set in this city. As Regina is not a big place, this is to be expected. I only found them when it was time to stock my bookstore. It is an odd and slightly disconcerting feeling to see references to familiar streets and landmarks in works of fiction. The feeling becomes weirder when the authors arrive in your shop to drink coffee and chat; I still harbour the belief that fiction writers are somehow Higher Beings. A fictionalised Regina is home to two teenaged, amateur detectives in Counios and Gane's *Shepherd and Wolfe* YA novels. It is also the setting for Suzy Krause's esoteric and humorous not-quite-ghost story, *Sorry I Missed You.* Suzy, Angie Counios and David Gane are all now regular customers of mine, and I am still star-struck whenever they come in.

It took a long time for those streets, fictionalised or not, to become familiar. Given that I have a doctorate degree in geography, and given my love of travelling, it has always been bitterly ironic that I have very little sense of direction. I can recognise places and remember them well—a coping strategy, perhaps—but I can neither navigate without explicit instructions, nor can I give people coherent directions. I also have a profound lack of spatial awareness, meaning that I am clumsy, and more significantly, I have never managed to pass my driving test. Therefore, I have always had to navigate Regina on foot, or by bike.

As a consequence, I did spend several weeks getting intentionally and unintentionally lost in Regina, as unused as I was to North American grid systems. Arriving in the spring allowed me to experience all of Saskatchewan's seasons in a few short weeks—a pattern I now know to be quite normal for this province. It snowed a few days after we landed in early April, which was quickly followed by the wet squelchy week where everything melted again, and then it all grew greener and greener until I got sunburnt at the end of the month. The greening of the city was beautiful to behold, as accustomed as I was to British concrete, clouds and cold. The streets are tree-lined, making them shady in summer and sheltered in winter, and stunning to look at the rest of the year.

Milo was at the age when, as we walked, every rock had to be stepped on, every pile of leaves jumped in, every squirrel or prairie dog admired or chased, and every streetlight pole twirled around. A journey of four blocks—our house to the coffee shop, for example—regularly took half an hour at Mini-Milo-Speed. Longer trips had to be planned ahead of time— does the number 15 bus go through that neighbourhood? Could I cycle this safely with Milo in the bike trailer? Was the building accessible with a giant stroller? All considerations that I would never have to contemplate if I was driving; yet deliberations that eventually led to a thorough exploration of the city.

In the UK, I used to navigate by meaningful local landmarks—in my case, this involved pubs and coffee shops as those are places I would naturally gravitate towards. In Sheffield, most sets of directions would start, "Go up the hill, past the pub on the corner ..." or "Get on the Crookes bus for five stops." Of course, there were actual road numbers and street names, but locals rarely used them. In Nicaragua, there are no street names and only the biggest, most important buildings have numbers. In Granada, the address of the hostel that I came to love so dearly literally translated to "the fourth house opposite where the water pump used to be, two blocks from the central park." Amazingly, this all worked because tourists were wholly reliant on taxi drivers who knew the local area intimately. In Sheffield, you only had to get on the right bus or tram and you'd usually end up approximately in the right place. But as a stranger in Regina, where public transit is lacking and having little knowledge how the streets intersected, I often found myself walking a great distance out of my way, thwarted by fenced off train tracks I did not expect, or accidentally going three sides around a square, confused by the grid system.

It's all far too logical for my European senses. I was as impressed with myself when I managed to get to a new place in Regina as I had been by my abilities to navigate in Nicaragua; both places were equally alien to me at first. But for once, I relished in it. This was my new, chosen home, and I wanted to soak it all in. For the first time, I was neither in a hurry to leave this new place nor limited by deadlines and flight times. I could afford to take life more slowly and fully appreciate my surroundings.

In those first few explorations of our new neighbourhood, I was delighted to find both a fantastic coffee roaster and cafe (Roca Jacks) and a used bookstore (Buy the Book) just a few blocks from my apartment in Regina, and I set about gradually replacing the books I had parted with during the Epic Move. Tragically for me, Buy the Book closed down just six months after I moved, and Roca Jacks followed soon after. This left the

Indigo-Chapters branch as the only mainstream bookstore in Regina. I went there once and bought a notebook with the words "Plans for World Domination" on the cover. In it I wrote, in 2013: *Both the bookshop and the coffee shop have closed down near me. Could this be an awesome opportunity? (Or is it a dire warning?)*

Warning or not, the seeds of an *idea* had been sewn.

7
A TALE OF TWO CITIES

It was the best of times, it was the worst of times, it
was the age of wisdom, it was the age of foolishness …

This quote is rather prescient, given Dickens wrote it in 1859. Like his fictionalised version of Paris, we seem to be living in an age of competing and contrasting attitudes. On one hand, science has produced a highly effective vaccine for a hitherto unknown virus in under two years. Billionaires are racing each other into space. Complicated new algorithm programming affects everything from helping make tweens famous on TikTok to alleviating supply chain issues at Christmas for my book distributors. And an AI Chatbot told its creator that it loved him.

At the same time, some people still need to be convinced that climate change is real and even that the earth isn't flat. In Regina, anti-mask mandate protestors were out demonstrating in the middle of winter—when it was so cold, they had to wear … ski masks. Most recently, people have been protesting adding fluoride to the water supply because obviously fluoridation is a government backed mind-control trick, or a communist plot to lower the IQs of our children. What a time to be alive!

We were tempted to rearrange our genres in the store to better reflect these extraordinary times, but instead decided to only put a sign up explaining the new categories:

The Travel section has been moved into Fantasy.
Apocalyptic fiction is now with Current Affairs.
Our Politics books are mixed in with the Horror section.
Epidemiology can be found amongst the Self-Help
and books on conspiracy theories are in the basement that we don't have.

Thankfully, most of our local customers appreciated the joke.

I do love Regina, but I often feel that I must explain or justify that statement. Regina is a provincial capital city that operates like a small town; it has both a strong sense of local pride, and yet everyone remains surprised that we would "choose" to move here. A happy accident brought us here but we definitely did well out of it. The city is just about big enough to go out and feel anonymous, but it is the first place I've ever lived where I actually know my neighbours. It is a wonderful place for our kids to grow up, and yet we fully accept that they will both probably leave the province at their earliest opportunity. At times I hate the local politics, but I know I would never have been able to create small businesses in the same manner anywhere else.

Regina is extremely flat. My favourite description of the city is from a friend in Saskatoon, who claims Regina looks like an empty parking lot with a pile of Lego in the middle. We get extremes of temperature every year - it can be 30 degrees Celsius at any point in the year, except sometimes that 30 has a minus sign in front of it. But what I love is the lack of rain. Having spent nearly 30 years in the UK, I cannot stand everything being constantly damp and miserable. I would rather have -40 and sunshine than it raining on Christmas Day. Saskatchewan gets, on average, 320 days of sunshine a year. My home town in the UK gets less than 80. Do we have solar power then? No, we don't. But perhaps that has as much to do with trenchcoated lobbyists from the fossil fuel industry attempting to influence government as it does long-term energy planning.

So, flatness, space and decent weather, I bet there's a great cycling culture, right?

Also no.

In truth, what divides the "two cities" of Regina is whether or not you view the place from a car window. In my neighbourhood, someone drives a bright yellow hummer four blocks to church every Sunday. The city is completely dominated by the "car," and that automobile is often a large pickup truck—the ubiquitous prairie vee-hickle. I do understand the need for these. That is, I understand the need for them if you are out in rural Saskatchewan, negotiating snow or towing cows or whatever people do with giant trucks out on farms. Few people actually need one in downtown Regina, yet they make up every other vehicle on the city streets.

Those roads are busy, the drivers impatient, the potholes craterous, and for six months or more, everyone drives on compressed snow. Public transport is sparse and inefficient after decades of underfunding so the default action of getting from A to B is to drive, and often drive a huge truck. As a result, drivers who fit that demographic have a fairly sweet ride, even if they do complain about paying for parking. Soon empty lots become "temporary" parking space and drivers create imaginary parking spots in areas marked as bus stops.

Cycle paths around the lake or between parks are designed for pretty little pleasure rides. They stop and start with no warning, don't join up with each other, and don't follow the regular commuter routes. The few bike lanes on the side of main roads are defined only by a mere line of paint; there is no barrier or any protection from cars. In the winter, sometimes the lanes disappear entirely when lanes are used as a handy place for the ploughs to dump great banks of snow. In the summer, cycling around Wascana Lake has different hazards. For some unfathomable reason, the sprinklers in the park are angled to water the asphalt and drench cyclists with cold lake water. Finally, if you do somehow make it downtown, the bike rack on the central, partially pedestrianised plaza has been installed *up a step*. At the time of writing, I am reading Suzanne Joinson's historical fiction novel, *A Lady Cyclist's Guide to Kashgar*. She writes: *The art of bicycling is a purely mechanical attainment; and though its complications may at first seem hopeless, sufficient practice will result in final mastery*. Although there is very little actual cycling in the book, I am beginning to think the lady cyclist in question had an easier time pedalling about in 1920s Western China than I do one hundred years later in Canada.

Despite all my complaining, I do really love cycling, even if my biking lifestyle comes more from necessity than desire. It is not that I won't drive, it's more that I really cannot. Driving both terrifies me and frustrates me because I know *theoretically* how to operate a car, I just can't physically do it. My spatial awareness is such that I have no concept of how long or wide the vehicle is so I invariably drive in the ditch or over the centre line, unsure of the car's position in the lane. I flinch whenever something passes us on multi-lane highways, even in the passenger seat, because it always looks as though we'll be sideswiped. No matter how many times Carl tries to talk me through reversing out of our garage, I just cannot visualise it. If you are a verbal learner like me, no amount of reading drivers' education textbooks can adequately prepare you for controlling a one-ton metal box at 110 km/hr.

My mother refers to my inability to drive, delightfully as ever, as "like having a disability," but to my mind that is far from the case. Not being able to drive around the city, compounded by my lack of sense of direction forces me to get creative. I am obligated to learn a city's transit system intimately, and I find the best cycle routes very quickly. Mercifully, my bookstore is now a comfortable walking or cycling distance from my house, but my non-driving stance has meant that I've learned the hard way how difficult cycle-commuting can be in Regina.

A guy honked his horn and yelled, "Get real!" at me as I cycled to my former workplace in the snow one morning, making me jump out of my skin. In my head, I responded: *You're an arsehole. What possible difference does it make to your day whether or not I cycle to work? You weren't even heading in the same direction, so it wasn't like I was in your way. I hope you skid and get stuck in a snowdrift.*

Get real: Whereas I don't expect random idiots to comprehend that some people don't want to drive, I'd hope that maybe they would understand that not everyone can afford to drive. For a long time, I fell into that category. Fuel costs, car maintenance, tax and insurance, and paying to park the car—long after the initial investment of buying one—all mean that I cannot justify having a car when neither I nor Carl have very far to go on a regular basis. We prefer to spend that money on more useful or fun things, and so biking is my transportation choice, even in the snow. (Sometimes, even public transport is not an option. For example, before my bookstore days, there was no bus that could actually get me to or from my work when I actually needed to travel.)

Get real. To my mind, cars are like cigarettes. They are highly addictive. Once you start driving, it is very difficult to break the habit of driving everywhere, all the time. I've seen all my friends who got their licences in their thirties do just that. We used to walk everywhere, pushing our kids in strollers. But now that their children are older, they drive, even a few blocks, because "it is just easier."

Get real. Cars are bad for you—as they stop you walking and biking—as well as bad for the whole planet. Statistically, driving is the most dangerous form of transport. Cars smell and pollute the air (like cigarettes). It is my fervent belief that in the not-too-distant future private car ownership will be looked back on with horror, as early cigarette adverts are today.

Until that change in society occurs, in Regina we have a totally inadequate cycling infrastructure to deal with, brutal winters, and screaming car-worshipping commuters. Annoyance fuels my sarcasm, and so as the guy in the truck accelerates away from me, I mentally compose the City of Regina's unwritten travelling advice for cyclists:

- Do not expect drivers to waste time looking for you. Wrap yourself in fairy lights at all times and sound an air horn as you travel.
- Know your place. Never inconvenience your superiors in cars by occupying the middle of the lane. Your place is in the gutter. To turn left, please levitate above the traffic.
- There is no situation where bikes ever have right of way.
- Re-examine your life choices at every intersection.
- For safety, consider travelling in a motorised metal box at all times.

Yes, I am bitter and cynical but I have been *doored*, yelled at, and squeezed off the road by truck drivers too many times. I don my helmet like a cloaking device, and for twenty minutes, I pedal myself into invisibility: an outcast, unseen and unwelcome.

But, soon enough, spring is here. I can smell it. Snow mould rises from the Melt, and there's a faint aroma of new plastic from my light rain jacket—it's all I needed this morning, and I even bought one with the bookstore's logo embroidered on it. The cold wind blasts my face, but today I revel in it as I am no longer hidden and blinkered at the sides by a frozen balaclava, nor half-strangled by a scarf. I am delivering books to happy customers, one of whom referred to me as a *Delivery Wizard*—which made my day.

I wobble down The Worst Road in the Cathedral neighbourhood. The snow that smothered it and smoothed out its potholes is gone too soon. Ice dams slowly crack into ruts too narrow for my wheels, leaving me weaving wildly, slipping and sliding and fishtailing along. My studded tyres try and fail to grip on the cleared trail that make this trip possible, passable, but unpleasant.

At the bridge over the still-frozen creek, I stop, get off and walk slowly, honouring a fallen fellow below: it is a grim sight. Half a bike, its wheels amputated, corpse like, laid out on a slab of ice on the morgue of the creek. Rigor mortis has set in and the chain, broken and splayed, will never turn again.

The path dips and I slip into a lower gear, brakes held tight down the slope, the box of books precariously balanced on the back. The fear of skids is all too real and the black ice forbids sharp cornering. So why do I ride so soon in the season? Why risk death by Dodge truck on those damaged and unfriendly roads? The desire to be outside is so strong, especially after a lockdown where every outing is curtailed and rationed. And it is only -4 today! Despite my numb, sore butt I feel the freedom of sunshine—I have been housebound too long, frozen through February, and caged in by cold since Christmas. Virus be damned: spring is here! I keep the faith that it can be "the best of times" again, and I am determined to enjoy it.

8
LANDLORDS AND OTHER PARASITES

It is 9 a.m. and the morning is glum. The sun has not fully risen; the ice on the inside of the shop window dims the view even more than the traffic's exhaust fumes outside of it. Disposable masks, once blue, now damp, muddy and grey, float down the street discarded in the breeze.

I flick on the lights, there is a flash and then the quick fizz of a bulb burning out. Dammit—it's the light directly above the seating area in the coffee bar. I love the lights in here—huge, heavy globes on long pendants, very mid-century modern—or so I'm told. Not something that's inexpensive to fix—each globe costs $120. Not something that's especially easy to fix either—the globes hang nine feet above my head. This is not a standing-on-a-chair type DIY operation.

It has been well over a month since my landlady had said a word to me, and I know asking her to fix the lights would be met with more icy silence at best. I sigh and move a table lamp to the top of the nearest head-height bookshelf.

There is a great literary tradition of the "Mad Woman in the Attic" trope. From Bronte's Mrs Rochester *(Jane Eyre)*, to Dickens' Miss Havisham *(Great Expectations)* and even Stella Gibbons' Ada Doom *(Cold Comfort Farm)*, these older, female characters—shunned and shut away in old buildings—are at the same time disturbing and tragic. Their malevolence can be felt throughout the novels, even if their presence is not immediately revealed.

My first bookish discovery of the vile old lady upstairs was in Joan Aiken's *Nightbirds on Nantucket*, where young Dido Twite lives in fear of her friend's aunt, who lives in the top room of an ancient and forlorn house on Nantucket isle. The girls refer to her as "Old Mortification." I read this when I was eight years old, and remember using the word *mortification* in a school project soon after. My young and extremely ginger teacher, Mr Robbins, was not sure if it was a real word and had to look it up.

Unfortunately, Aiken's forty-year-old, British, alternative history children's books are a bit of an obscure reference, especially to my Gen Z Canadian employees. Consequently, when we first encountered a real *Vile Old Lady in the Attic* at the Penny, I couldn't get "Old Mortification" to stick. Instead, we shall call her "Sylvia."

After nine years of renting residential and commercial property in Regina, I have to conclude that the city has some of the worst landlords I've ever had the misfortune to deal with. It is only very recently that I have entered the Property Ownership state of being. I am now Winning At Capitalism and have a certificate to prove it. (The certificate reads *Mortgage Statement* on the top of the first page.)

I have been at the mercy of Saskatchewan landlords long enough to learn that the landlord-tenant relationship is much less equal here than in the UK. Not to say that British landlords are wonderful, they certainly are not, but the UK tenant seems to have considerably more power. In spite of an act written to protect both landlords and tenants, The Residential

Tenancies Act of Saskatchewan seems to imply that the tenant should simply "put up and shut up." I'm stumped as to why that is. Houses are much bigger here, and there are fewer people. The geographical crampedness of the British isles coupled with acute population density would suggest that conditions would be worse over there, as there is so much competition for decent housing. Regina is the provincial capital and the prices reflect that, but you do get what you pay for (if only in comparison with the UK). The same is not true of the bigger Canadian cities where you must be a multi-millionaire to buy a dog kennel, so maybe the abundance of space and relative affordability of Saskatchewan has to be balanced by the callousness of the property owners?

Landlord the First, in our first rented house in this country, refused to return our deposit because we hadn't cleaned the house "to his standards" when we left. I did point out that two days before we were supposed to move out, I was in hospital miscarrying my baby. Somehow after that tragedy, I wasn't really concentrating on cleaning. Apparently, there are few grounds for compassionate flexibility in Saskatchewan's Tenancies Act, however.

Landlord the Second, a well-heeled woman with one of those sports cars that looks like it's been sat on, and who insisted on capitalizing the second *syllable* of her name, was no more friendly. Annoyed that after two years, we did not want to buy the house from her, she withheld our deposit —money that we were relying on to offset the legal fees of arranging our first mortgage elsewhere. We took her to a rentalsman tribunal. She didn't show up to the hearing, so we won by default. She still didn't return the money. We received a court judgement ordering her to pay. She ignored the judgement. We got the Sheriff's office involved. She blocked their phone calls.

We put a lien on the rental house and then found out that she had not been paying the mortgage, or any property taxes. The bank eventually foreclosed on the house and sold it off at auction for a quarter of its market value. Unfortunately, that was not enough to cover the remaining mortgage and her outstanding property taxes, so her much smaller debt to us was a long way down the list, and we didn't see a penny.

Three and a half years after we moved out of that rental, I was contacted by a stranger who found me via the Information Services Commission. He claims that this woman also owed him $88,000 after fraudulent business dealings and he wanted me to be a co-plaintiff when he sued her. He even employed a Private Investigator to find out where she was living! We are approaching year seven of the Landlady Saga, and now the RCMP are involved as well. I have received a Christmas card from the Sheriff's office four years in a row.

I'm sure there is a noir novel in this, albeit a rather farcical one. We've got a classy, colourful antagonist, multiple victims, espionage and intrigue, and a jaded, world-weary PI in a fedora (no doubt battling alcoholism) but insisting on one last case. I'm making a few assumptions here, granted. There's even the honest, but over-worked, Sheriff. All the novel requires is a good rainstorm and a gritty jazz soundtrack. The ultimate irony and twist to be revealed at the end of this drama is that our landlady actually works as a realtor! The plot thickens ... would you buy a house from a character like this? Who will fall prey to her charms next?

My first commercial landlord—when leasing space for my first Regina coffee shop—was not exactly hostile or unpleasant. He was the sort of nondescript bloke you'd expect to see propping up a bar in any friendly local boozer the world over. His name really was "Dave." And because this provincial capital is such a small town, I found out afterwards that he was also the deadbeat Dad to my friend's toddler.

Dave was just dimwitted. I will never understand why he chose to buy that building - at a police auction, no less. The place was raided and seized when an (at the time) illegal cannabis grow-op had been discovered in its basement. At least one member of the family that owned it was jailed, but the rest continued to run other businesses in Regina, unperturbed by the loss and sale of their building. Dave acquired it very cheaply but knew nothing about being a landlord. Unfortunately for us, whenever his ignorance was revealed, he would go on the defensive and have temper tantrums that lasted for a few days and then would never be mentioned again. We learned to live with it after a while, but my accounts ledger from the cafe tell a sorrier tale. There were two other tenants in the building, one on each floor, and so Dave's idea for handling the utility bills was to just divide everything by three. Except he couldn't do the math well. Every few months, I'd have an entry in the expenses book to match a "corrected" utility bill: *$17.43 to Saskpower, Reason: Dave's a dumbass.*

As landlords go, dumbasses are bearable, but the final straw came when Dave sold the building from under us, not realizing that this would nullify our leases. Amusingly, he sold it back to the grow-op family who had originally owned it. Not wanting to negotiate a new lease with a stranger who we assumed would be more competent and therefore more expensive, we took this as our cue to leave. A huge poster of Bob Marley covers the entire window of my former coffee shop. Inside, I can safely say it is the most attractive grow-op in Regina.

Maybe it's my tenacity, or merely my inability to afford to buy property, but none of these experiences seem to have put me off leasing spaces for my ventures. I genuinely thought 2020 would be full of jokes about perfect vision. As it turns out, I do have 2020 vision, but only in my hindsight.

My next landlord, the aforementioned Sylvia, would not make a plausible character in a novel, not even in a suspenseful type of *Vile Old Lady in the Attic* gothic horror. As an author, I cannot conjure up her motivation. She is spiteful for the sake of spite, manipulative with no end game, and she never directly benefited from any of the mean little tricks she inflicted on us. She never became a well-rounded character to us because her intentions were unfathomable. Every baddie needs a tragic flaw to be believable, a catalyst to set cruel events in motion. Without this, Sylvia remains a cardboard cut-out, pantomime villain in this story. "Watch out! She's behind you!"

In November 2019, I met Sylvia, a short woman in her sixties, with quite an edgy undercut in her thick grey hair, little round glasses, and a shapeless black t-shirt. She took me on a tour of her leasable space while her elderly mother sat in the corner, watching us unnervingly. The building was huge, right on one of the main arteries of the city and therefore highly visible but still affordable. A big window at "car-height" would be excellent for displays, I thought, and it had a pre-built bathroom and kitchen, perfect for doing coffee along with the books.

"What sort of business are you planning?" Sylvia inquired as I wiped the snow off my boots and the steam from my glasses.

"Oh, a *bookshop*!" she cooed excitedly to my response. "That would be wonderful!"

By the end of January 2020, I had found start-up funding, and had a preliminary lease arranged with Sylvia. At that time, Covid-19 was a brief news story, buried under the catastrophic pictures of the Australian wildfires and the latest Trumpian outrage from south of the border. And I knew nothing of Sylvia's "Mrs Rochester" tendencies.

On March 11th, 2020, I met Sylvia at the building and she presented me with the official lease document.

Reader, I signed it.

On March 16th, 2020, Saskatchewan declared a state of emergency from the Covid-19 pandemic.

9
L SPACE AND THE GARAGE PROBLEM

In the early spring of 2020, the whole world gradually shut down around us. My bookish endeavours, and even my brand-new lease, suddenly dropped from my priority list as the schools closed, and the daycare begged every parent who was not an essential worker to keep their children at home to keep places for the most in need. Milo and Theia welcomed the time at home at first. Finally, my husband's office shut down and he was sent to work from home as well. The streets emptied, but our house filled up.

And then we had the Garage Problem.

The Garage Problem manifested itself as a result of my optimism and over-ambition regarding the bookstore, and my underestimating of the pandemic. As soon as I signed the lease, I began to *prepare* for the opening. What that really means is that I spent considerable amounts of borrowed money buying books. The Premier of Saskatchewan naively said "a couple of weeks of lockdown" should do the trick. Perfect timing to buy all the stock, I thought, so I had it ready to go when all this coronavirus fuss had blown over.

To this end, and never being a fan of round numbers, I ordered 982 books. At the virtual checkout, I had a choice between "Use company's preferred shipping" or "Use my own courier." Having no concept of what 982 books looked like in physical volume, I chose their shipping method. About two weeks later, a huge truck—a semi-trailer—attempted to back into the alley down the side of our house. My first thought was that someone was moving into the house across the street. Then came a tap on the door. A young man in a white "Jay's Transport" shirt told me, "We've got your ... boxes, ma'am." Clearly, the driver had no idea what he was delivering. At that point, I had no idea what I was signing to receive either.

982 books take up seventeen, 40-pound boxes.

Now, anyone with half a brain would have thought: *That's a lot of boxes! You should stack them straight in the garage until you can sort through them!* But no, at that precise moment my brain simply disengaged and I said, "Oh just dump them in the hall, that will be fine." Ten minutes later, I could no longer get out of the front door, or up the stairs to the second floor. This was not "fine."

I was on my own at the time of the momentous delivery and I suddenly panicked, thinking that Carl would despair of me if he came home to find I'd blocked the entrance way with all these books. So, I began to carry them out to the garage by myself.

Did I mention they weighed 40 *pounds* each? I can lift 40 lb easily enough, but *only* 40 lb. I couldn't stack the boxes on top of each other and still carry them the length of the house, down the back steps and across the yard. So, I had to do seventeen trips. It was one hell of a work out!

It did not end at seventeen boxes. By the end of April, even the most optimistic of us had realised that the coronavirus was not to be a mere short-term inconvenience. I stopped buying books because I now had no idea when I could open the bookshop—if ever. Prior to the pandemic, before even signing the lease on the building, I had been in touch with a local publisher, a stalwart of the Saskatchewan literary scene who published books by authors all over Canada and had been in business for forty-five years. They were housed just two blocks away from where the bookstore would eventually open, and I had contacted them eagerly hoping to stock their titles. Initially, around Christmas 2019, they had been very receptive and excited about finally having a local stockist.

However, not for the first time in my entrepreneurial career, I felt ghosted. Meetings with the publisher never happened, phone calls trailed off, emails failed to materialise and as the spring dawned, I resorted to marching downtown in my snow boots to visit the office in person. The front window of their building is deceptively small, and gave no clue as to the sheer size of their warehoused collection stretching back from the street. Through the window I was accustomed to seeing the single publicist sitting in his office surrounded by piles of paper. He had a cheery piece of sage advice for would-be authors taped to the glass of the front door window that read: *Keep typing until it turns into writing.*

On that day though, the advice was gone, and so was the man in the office. Instead, taped on the outside of the locked door, was an official bankruptcy notice. This did not bode well. The demise of the publisher was not another pandemic casualty, as the company had obviously been in trouble for some considerable time before this notice appeared. This, I decided, must be a test of my nerve. Did I dare continue with my bookstore venture, knowing that even a place with such a long and illustrious history couldn't survive?

But then, I realised the very reason I had contacted them in the first place was because it *did* survive. And flourish. For forty-five years. If my business survives for forty-five years, I will be very happy indeed. To get to that point, however, I had to build it now.

The death of a publisher is a tragic, yet intriguing affair. A few interesting emails and some research later, and I had managed to contact one of the former board members of the publishing company. My question was simple but important: what happens to all the books when a publisher closes? The answer: a public auction. The receiver had first offered the books to the authors, but there are very few authors who wanted several hundred copies of their own book. Some took a few copies, most just gave up and, having reclaimed the rights to their work, reluctantly began the search for a new publisher elsewhere.

What was left was a warehouse, lined floor to ceiling with boxes and boxes and boxes of books. Depending on the thickness of the book, each box contained 20 to 50 copies of the same title. There were hundreds of titles stretching back over the company's long history. Interested parties were invited to have a look in the warehouse to see what was available, but, due to Covid, the auction itself took place entirely online.

The books were cheap—depressingly so, given the work that had obviously gone into them. But the miniscule price came with a caveat: you couldn't bid on individual books, you had to buy the box of 30 or more copies. There was little information about the books, just the title, author name, the number of copies of the title in the box, and a thumbnail picture of the cover. I would have appreciated even the vaguest of descriptions, but as it was, I had to judge these books by their covers alone. I had studied the publisher's latest catalogue and had a good idea of their most recent titles, but acquiring information on the older books would have meant physically rooting through those boxes, which none of the bidders at the auction had the opportunity to do.

On auction day, I recognised the usernames of a few authors already online making bids and left those boxes well alone—I did not want to outbid the people who had actually written the books! I soon discovered I was also bidding along with the owner of a new-and-used bookstore in

Moose Jaw, and the owner of Spafford Books, a hidden gem in Regina that sells antiquarian and specialist books. The owner of Spafford Books was mainly after the art and Saskatchewan history titles. There were plenty of boxes to go around though, and I think all of us ended up with sizable collections.

A week after the auction, we went to pick up our winnings. Yet again, I underestimated the physical space that this quantity of books takes up. For an extremely reasonable sum of money, I had managed to acquire another 42 boxes of books, around 2400 individual novels, and unlike my previous order, this time I really didn't know what I'd actually bought. I convinced Carl to drive us over to the warehouse and shoved as many boxes as we could in the back of his minivan. Strangely, forty-two boxes do not fit in one vehicle with two adults and two kids already inside but the pandemic meant babysitters were in short supply and so the kids had to come along for the ride.

I had begged Sylvia to let me store some of these book boxes in the building of the would-be bookstore and about a third of my auction boxes were stacked along the stairs at the back of the building before Sylvia commanded us to stop unloading. The other two-thirds ended up in our garage, along with my first seventeen boxes.

This, I assumed, was not an unmanageable situation; as we weren't really going anywhere during the lockdown, the car did not need to be moved in and out the garage constantly, and there was still room for me to squeeze my bike out if I needed to escape. Furthermore, having them all stacked up in one place would allow me to figure out what was in each box and organise them neatly, all ready for placing them on my brand-new shelves. At least, that's what I told myself.

There is a strange magic to books, and I was oddly thrilled whenever I thought about the sheer quantity of them in the garage. The bookstore was starting to feel more real, too. I knew I shouldn't open the boxes and go rifling through them because it would make it far harder to move them into the shop, but I was itching to have a look. The whole of the outside world was paused, but in the newly formed garage-library, a cosy, surreal little space was forming and I was excited.

Maybe it's a result of too much *Discworld* at a formative age, but after a few weeks of living wedged between boxes of books, I began to feel uneasy. Eventually, I started to attribute it to the phenomenon of "L-space." In Terry Pratchett's magnificent *Discworld* series, *L-space*, short for *library-space*, is the ultimate portrayal of Pratchett's concept that the written word has powerful magical properties and that, in large quantities, books will warp space and time around them. The principle of L-space revolves around a seemingly logical premise: *Knowledge is Power*—books contain knowledge, and therefore, they must be powerful. But *power* can be converted to energy, and energy into matter. And that's how L-space is created.

In the *Discworld*, piles of books stored together, be they magical or mundane, create portals into L-space that can be accessed using the innate powers of librarianship by those deemed worthy across the multiverse. Because libraries with enough books to open a portal are often large and sprawling, those venturing into L-space may not necessarily know that they have arrived. The floor and ceiling of L-space follow the floor and ceiling of the library used to access it; in my case, the uninsulated chipboard walls of our garage, lined with boxes of my books stretching out in every direction.

I make no pretence of being a librarian, however, or having the powers to open portals. Alternatively, I like to imagine that L-space manifests in our world in those obscure, hidden bookstores that, logic and the laws of physics insist, cannot possibly be as large on the outside as they appear on the inside. When pandemic stress subsided enough for me to fantasise and be silly (not a frequent occurrence, sadly), this was my dream store design. Of course, I would have to have an improbably tiny door to create this effect—something I am averse to given I am awkwardly tall—but then my customers would find themselves turning from one unseen corner after another, seemingly going on forever into further and more obscure sections as yet unobserved by human eyes.

Furthermore, Pratchett explains, by the very nature of words themselves, every book ever written contains the building blocks of every other book that ever *could be* written. Books are self-replicating. Essentially, my store could be infinite in size and capacity, as the sheer mass of words in those boxes could bend reality and potentially extend our garage forever. It was a wonderful fantasy, unless you thought it through too carefully.

Taking the boxes of books out of the publisher's warehouse had only moved the cosmic warp to my house, it had not diminished the books' power. If books could stretch time and space, and if my collection could be rendered infinite by this, how on earth would I sell them all, and how would we ever clear out the garage?

It was a sobering thought. And I eventually gave in, and opened some of the boxes.

At this point, we were in a full lockdown, nowhere to go, nothing to do and no hope of company outside of a Zoom screen. Although Carl was able to work from home and his income kept us fairly comfortable, I was not working in any paid capacity: childcare and impromptu home education are obviously not lucrative endeavours. I was also not eligible for CERB, the Canadian Emergency Response Benefit, as I had left my previous job voluntarily before the pandemic hit. I decided it was time to try and make some money and build up my customer base before The Grand Opening, whenever that would be.

I had no catalogue of the books, merely the receipt for the first 982 items that listed the book by title alone, and the long list of Lot numbers that I had "won" at the auction. I had no way of communicating what was available to my potential customers, and even if they had asked for something specific, I would have difficulties finding one title in the mass of unlabelled boxes. So, in keeping with my magical, fantastical and slightly disturbing collection, I decided to sell 'surprise" books. Customers would give me a general idea of what they liked to read, and I would find something appropriate in L-space and deliver it to them on my bike.

Over time, we began to move in the L-space differently, especially as the weather warmed up and we were outdoors more often. We got quite used to stepping sideways into the garage, as book boxes prevented us from opening the door fully. As we were no longer using the kids' sleds in the spring, those were soon buried behind boxes too. Carl's workbench and tool kit were no longer accessible at all. The car occupied a very narrow strip of space, but the boxes lining each side prevented Theia from getting into the one side of the car, requiring her to climb across from the opposite door. I regularly had to lift my bike over the boxes because one of the stacks fell and we decided it was safer to keep them all at floor height, just in case a true accident occurred. Initially, Carl found this garage situation far more stressful and frustrating than I did, and I am eternally grateful for his patience. After a while, however, I too became anxious, but for a different reason. It was a constant and very physical reminder of the predicament I could be in if I never managed to get the store open.

So accustomed were we to this cramped and irritating existence, that we kept only opening the door halfway, kept only using one side of the car and automatically stepped over boxes long after I had begun moving and emptying them. This led to the unwelcome discovery of a new phenomenon—boxes that had always been there, *but that weren't there yesterday*. With a determined effort one day, I exhausted myself hauling boxes about and putting them in some semblance of order, just to keep myself sane. I knew roughly where the few boxes containing nonfiction history books from my first order were, and I knew that the four auction boxes containing most of the *Shards of Excalibur* fantasy series by Edward

Willett were stacked beside my bike. Kids' books were the ones by the door, and my mystery and thriller boxes were blocking the side of the car.

Why then, when I came in to find a book for someone who said they liked Nordic noir, did I trip over a box that I swear—*knew*—hadn't been in that location last time I came in, but had all the same squashed edges and torn packing tape as the ones that we had been climbing around and over for months? And why, when I opened it, did it happen to contain ten copies of *I'm Travelling Alone* by Norwegian novelist Samuel Bjork? Exactly what I needed! I put it down to pandemic stress—I must have forgotten I had left it there. Of course, I would have ordered some Scandi-Crime at some point. Eventually, I convinced myself I had seen that title on my receipt.

The "Little Shop That Wasn't There Yesterday" is a literary trope that pops up in many different genres. Those little places that somehow, you've never noticed before, and that conveniently stock the exact item you need, or didn't know you needed, at exactly the right time. The items are usually cursed, and yet if you try and return to get a refund, you can never find the place again. In literature, Pratchett used this idea in *The Light Fantastic*, but it harks back to the weird fantasy of the 1920s and earlier: H.G. Wells used it in his books *The Crystal Egg* and *The Magic Shop*. Most recently, I came across the same trope in *Pyjama Day* by Robert Munsch when reading it for Theia's bedtime story. The little shop contains magic "perfect" pyjamas that cause the kid wearing them to fall asleep instantly. I wish I could find perfect pyjamas for my kids.

My adventures in this odd and unnerving L-space continued all summer, as the world became a stranger and stranger place around me. Brief outings delivering the books did break up the malaise of lockdown however, and the surprise book packages were very popular, probably because I was distracting and amusing my customers as well as myself. I did seem to develop a knack of picking books for people quickly, and my customers were often highly appreciative of my choices. Maybe it was just luck, or maybe something more fantastical, but given the narrow range of books I had in the garage, the surprise aspect should have been more difficult to get right each time. If I'm honest, I was shocked by how well it all worked.

Books are magical things.

10
QUARANTINE READS

Being cramped is not fun. Throughout the early days of the pandemic when lockdowns were in full force, when people were scared—and as it seems in hindsight, actually taking the threat of Covid-19 seriously—suddenly being confined to the house came as a shock to many of us. Working from home was one thing, working from home when your spouse was also working from home caused a lot of friction. Working from home with your partner and your bored, worried kids was more stressful than many of us could have imagined. It did very odd things to my psyche.

I am sure I am not alone in feeling like my house shrank. Too many bodies taking up space, children's clutter everywhere, and the smells! Little things you'd never normally notice slowly wormed their way into your consciousness: I had little concept of how much cheese on toast my husband would consume when he had access to a grill during the work day. Mixed in with toasting cheese were the ubiquitous pandemic fragrances of hand sanitiser and Lysol wipes, combined with the general odour of our pets.

Eventually, the sounds that usually contributed to a comforting background noise became a source of constant irritation. The music in the Splatoon video game will haunt me forever as the soundtrack to the pandemic. New noises joined them too: Carl found a plea from health care workers in Michigan in desperate need of face shields and ear protectors to wear with masks. We own a 3D printer and Carl set the machine up to be constantly printing these. He diligently mailed piles of ear protectors and face shields out to hospitals in the US, and every night we would go to sleep listening to the irregular whine of the print head moving back and forth downstairs. After a while it began to sound like strange alien singing.

These new circumstances were certainly not the sort of world-changing phenomenon that I had read about in speculative fiction novels or watched in my husband's favourite disaster movies. I was almost disappointed. It was far slower-moving and less dramatic than books had taught me to expect, and the kids maintained that they would probably die of boredom before they died of plague. If we consider the dystopian fiction of old, few authors accurately predicted how this form of apocalypse would play out. That fiction was all far too proactive and energetic and involved too much running away from zombies. In his trilogy in five parts, *The Hitchhiker's Guide To The Galaxy*, Douglas Adams did have his hero wearing pyjamas when the Earth was destroyed, but I don't know of a single book where humans actually saved the world by loafing about at home ... and reading.

But that is exactly what we could all do. There was really no better time to try and read Lucy Ellmann's *Ducks, Newburyport*—a thousand-page novel comprising of one sentence. As we merrily passed the second anniversary of Covid-19's discovery, hindsight would suggest that we could have done wonders if we'd spent a little longer cosying up at home with a good book, and not exacerbating the situation by opening up too early. We now have a considerable amount of data about these strange pandemic days and there are some fascinating trends that I did not see coming.

As previously explained, the spring of 2020 found me with a few thousand books inhabiting my garage. While not particularly comfortable, we resigned ourselves to the arrangement given we were still in the midst of a global pandemic. The whole world was crazy, so a garage full of books was nothing to really worry about. It also had some advantages.

By this point, I was on a lot of mailing lists from the publishing industry, and many emails were devoted to analysing trends in book buying. Most mirrored my meagre experience: people were finally getting to their "Books to be Read" piles and reading more. The Black Lives Matter movement was fuelling an interest in activist literature and plenty of memoirs and social commentary books from black writers. People were looking for cookbooks, particularly with recipes using sourdough. Those stuck in urban apartment blocks, staring out the window all day, suddenly demanded books on bird spotting. The beginnings of a strong "shop local" trend benefitted independent bookstores. Most interestingly, and unexpectedly, many of these industry updates mentioned that sales of audiobooks had drastically decreased since the pandemic began. This, they reasoned, was because few people were travelling to work anymore, whereas they used to listen to audiobooks while commuting.

Books about plagues were understandably very polarising at the time. Based on my requests from customers alone (rather than things I chose to stock myself), some either wanted something so horrible that the real world would seem a nicer place in comparison, or they wanted light, adventurous escapism reads. We did not have many requests for what I would loosely label "beach reads" because no one needed the reminder that they had been forced to cancel their summer holidays.

I picked up a copy of *Quarantine* by Jim Crace in a Free Library just before the-Christmas-before-Covid-19, and given the title, I thought that March was the perfect time to read it. It has absolutely nothing to do with global pandemics but everything to do with being isolated with a small group of desperate people. It explores Jesus's forty days of fasting in the wilderness, along with six other companions who are all enduring "quarantine" in an effort to find healing. It is cruel, bleak, and utterly captivating—and made my own quarantining experience seem positively luxurious in comparison.

One rather ironic thriller that I had stocked without understanding its relevance, was *2020* by Kenneth Stevens. Steven's slim novella is set in a not-very-United Kingdom. Apparently written just *before* the 2016 Brexit referendum, the depiction of a violently divided country is horrifyingly accurate in reflection of the present day. I had numerous copies of it, and as we re-opened in the new year of 2021, we ceremoniously placed a copy in a garbage bin and displayed it in our window.

As well as reading, people were binge-watching Netflix. I was asked to source several books with TV tie-ins. I think I've only ever sold one set of the Bridgerton novels, but they were certainly very much in the public consciousness as a non-challenging form of escapism. I had many requests for *American Gods* and *Good Omens* as a result of the TV adaptations that came out around the same time, and I was happy to introduce people to the wonders of Neil Gaiman. Sci-fi fans were treated to the first seasons of James S. A. Corey's *The Expanse*, a futuristic saga with so many political subplots that I struggled to keep up even with the abbreviated TV episodes. (A few customers, attempting to read all eight thick hardcovers once they learned that the series came in print form, told me the storylines are easier to follow in the books.)

In preparation for opening the shop, I read *The Bookseller* by Cynthia Swanson, where the lead character is torn between the need to stay home and look after her kids, or follow her dreams and open her bookstore. That was a little too close to home for my liking. Then, there was *The Bookshop* by Penelope Fitzgerald (made into a film in 2017). My mum actually bought me a copy for my birthday in February just as I had accepted the business loan. Knowing that she usually reads everything she gives me first, I wondered at the choice, especially as it ends with the line: *As the train drew out of the station, she sat with her head bowed in shame, because the town she had lived in for nearly ten years had not wanted a bookshop.*

Ouch.

Finally, I read *The Revenge of Analog* by David Sax. I wanted to hate this one because it is the sort of book that makes you feel inadequate for not wearing flannel and mispronouncing *charcuterie*. But, in a time of renewed interest in traditional crafts and where "slow" is paramount, I feel we need a book exploring the resurgence of independent bookstores and vinyl record shops, and the joys of Moleskine notebooks and board games.

Perhaps the most useful book I read had nothing to do with books or bookselling. It was *Everything is F*cked* by Mark Manson, with the subtitle: *A Book About Hope.* Along with many other philosophical debates, Manson explores the premise that a hero is not someone who does heroic deeds, but a person who, against all evidence to the contrary, remains hopeful for a better world and tries to make it happen. The ability to retain hope and keep faith in humanity in desperate times is an admirable skill, and one that I truly wish to cultivate.

One day, I took Theia to the bookstore building, armed with window marker pens. *The Penny University Bookstore is coming soon!* I wrote on the window. *Until then, Help Save the World: Stay Home and Read.*

11
NO

After nearly three years running The Penny University Bookstore, I am finally able to look at what we've created and feel proud. It really is a lovely little space, and one that I feel very at home in. It is also very colourful, which seems to be a signature feature of my ventures. One comment about the bookstore that we received online has always baffled me, though. Someone complimented us on the shop and said, "It's so nice to see a children's section that looks like a children's section." I am still none-the-wiser as to what it would look like if it *didn't* look like a children's section, but overall, I am quite happy with our bright, cheerful corner. The kid's corner is lined with a large alphabet mat in primary colours, a small table topped with a dry erase board that kids can draw on, and of course, low shelves to hold all the books.

Occasionally some of those books come with special toys attached, but for the most part, it's books, books and more books. I am very conscious of which children's books make it onto the shelves: nothing with TV tie-ins, nothing Disney, nothing written entirely with the aim of selling more toys. Of course, some childrens' books are made into movies and so movie-related merchandise is inevitable: Harry Potter being the obvious example, and there are hundreds of Winnie the Pooh and Paddington stuffies available, some of which eventually did find their way into my store but in all these cases, the books came first.

This reluctance to carry toys for toys' sake may sound snobbish—and it is—but it comes from a deep-rooted loathing of over-priced plastic dolls. The pandemic brought home to me poignantly what goes through the mind of a four-year-old child with nowhere to go and no one except Mum and her dolls to hang out with.

When the lockdown began in Saskatchewan, I thought we were lucky, in comparison with some. I was at home anyway. I hadn't actually opened the bookstore only to have it closed down again immediately, so I was "free" to look after the kids in the absence of school and daycare. Carl could easily work from home. We were more or less financially secure. We were healthy. And we were all together. But this did not mean for a second that our circumstances were entirely positive and cheery, and as the lockdown wore on, I found myself saying "No" more and more frequently.

"Stay away from Daddy's new office!" was a common refrain. (By which I meant the computer desk in the dining room.) We do not have a home office, in fact most of the ground floor of our house is open plan. This had never been an issue before, as we'd never needed to shut each other out of the shared space. Now, the computer area has become a battleground.

"No, we can't go to the playground!" (In early April 2020, the Government of Saskatchewan closed down all the outdoor play structures for fear of the Covid-19 virus being spread by kids touching common surfaces like slides and swing chains.) It was very difficult explaining this one to Theia, whose first thought was that as the nearest playground was closed, we should go to "the big one by the river." (Theia maybe the only person in Regina who refers to the stinky creek that leads into Wascana Lake as a 'river.') It took considerable effort to convince her that we didn't just mean one park was closed, but that ALL the parks were closed.

The situation soon worsened.

"No, no playdates, sorry. We can't see your friends right now."

"No, you can't go on the neighbour's trampoline. No, I know it's HUMONGOUS, but we're not allowed to visit at the moment."

And then came the dolls.

"No, go play by yourself. Mummy doesn't like LOL dolls. I don't care if they want to do a fashion show." (LOL Dolls are a toy brand where the dolls arrive in opaque eggs, wrapped in a ludicrous amount of plastic, with special "surprises" between each layer of wrapping until you find the doll in the center. The dolls are only about three inches high, and so each accessory is impossibly tiny and instantly lost as soon as it is dropped on the rug.)

"No, I don't know where its shoes are. Okay, okay, I'll change its dress. There you go. Are you going to clear up all this glitter they've dropped?"

"No, I don't know where Cosmic Nova is. Isn't that her on the floor? No, I'm sorry, I don't know the difference. Oh, Cosmic Nova has blue hair, so who is this pink one?"

"No, you can't play on the tablet—Milo's using it for school."

"Why don't you play with Milo? No? Have you asked? I'm sure Milo would like to play dolls far more than Mummy would."

"No! Don't shout up the stairs! Just go up and ask nicely!"

Off she stomps, and inside I am torn. Do other mothers crawl around on the floor playing with pink plastic dolls with oversized eyes and no noses? Am I a terrible parent for not wanting to? Why do these deformed-looking figures fill me with so much irrational hatred?

She reappears, heartbroken and sobbing.

"Milo said No! Mummy, just play with me! You have to play!"

Her desperation is too much, and all of a sudden, I am kneeling uncomfortably on the floor, walking a pink glittery doll around. They are apparently going swimming, which also means I must immediately fetch a bowl of water with ice cubes in it, because the dolls change colour in icy water.

"I miss swimming, Mummy."

"I know you do, darling."

I am lucky—I get to spend time with my daughter. I am lucky. I get to be Mum, teacher, source of entertainment—and her only friend.

She's happy now: "Mummy, you be Bee Queen. We are at the pool! Yay! But we can't get too close or touch cos we will get sick…"

And now, I'm the heartbroken one.

12
THE FLOOR TILES OF DORIAN GRAY

In early May 2020, a CBC van appeared outside my house, and a small crew wearing latex gloves set up a microphone on a stand in front of my overstuffed garage. They cleaned the microphone with a disinfecting wipe, but then realised they also needed a sound boom as the microphone did not carry my voice sufficiently outdoors. Due to the mandated six-foot social-distancing measures, they kept away from where I would be standing, thrusting the sound boom in my face from a distance. The sound boom eventually had to be propped up inelegantly using my recycling bin to support the extra length of its pole.

Two hours beforehand, the Premier of Saskatchewan and the Chief Medical Officer had announced Saskatchewan's grand re-opening plan. This plan had five stages, staggering the re-opening of businesses after lockdown so we couldn't pour back to our "normal" lives all at once. It was highly experimental though, as we were the first province in Canada to attempt lifting Covid-19 restrictions. CBC had contacted me as someone whose business plan had been severely affected by the lockdown to get my reaction to the morning's announcements.

This would have been considerably easier for me if I'd known where to watch the announcement so I would have a better idea of what I was expected to react to. I had diligently turned on CBC television at 10 a.m. to find only children's programming with overly chirpy hosts and Margaret Atwood's new literacy cartoon show *Wandering Wenda*. No news program. CTV and Global gave me nothing either. I frantically texted some media-savvy friends and was told that the announcement was on Facebook Live. I rarely check my Facebook account nor do I have the app that would allow me to watch live, so I was stumped. I never thought for a moment that an official government announcement like this would be relegated to social media! Not exactly the most accessible way to convey important information. Fortunately, Carl was home and logged in with his Facebook account, and I managed to catch the end of the broadcast.

I learned then that I would be allowed to open my retail business on May 19th in Phase 2 of the plan (after golf courses—*obviously*). As coffee shops and restaurants were in Phase 3 (and no date had been set for those as of yet), I would be able to sell books, but not serve coffee. There was also no date for when the schools would re-open. Suddenly, I was annoyed. I decided then and there that I would not be opening on May 19th, even if the powers that be had deemed it safe. There were other factors to consider.

Fortunately, the interviewer gave me the opportunity to vent my frustrations on national television. I made sure that this interview was actually being broadcast on television and not on Facebook, and was told that after editing, it would go out that evening on The National. I was, and remain ever grateful for, the "after editing" phrase. I am not the best public speaker.

I used the word "obliterated" to describe what the pandemic had done to my business plans, which might have been a tad overdramatic, but the fear was still very real at that point. I muttered something about being pleased to see the province set a date for re-opening, but then tried to explain that the continuing restrictions on daycare could further delay my opening. Daycare centres were still limited to a maximum of eight children, and I had chosen to keep Theia at home because I was in the position to be able to do so, in the hope that the eight places could be used by the offspring of essential workers instead. The schools remained closed indefinitely, and so I still had Milo to look after as well.

"It's a big consideration, particularly for very small businesses, if you are a parent ... it restricts you a lot, what you can do," I said, only semi-coherently. "Anyone who is working from home is still struggling to look after kids—to keep them entertained and happy—and work as well. It's not like they magically disappear as soon as businesses start re-opening again."

This was the source of my frustration. It felt as though all safety concerns for children and families had simply been ignored as a minor inconvenience as soon as the government had decided we needed to be economically productive again. There were so many wholesome posts online cheering on all the mums who had suddenly become home-educators, and the parents juggling all the unexpected new responsibilities of quarantine—but they all rang a little hollow to me. Whereas it was nice to be thanked occasionally, some actual logistical or financial support would have been far more welcome! I chose entrepreneurship because it gives me more flexibility when it comes to childcare than a regular corporate job would, but I still rely heavily on schools and daycare. If the lockdown taught me anything, it's that looking after my two beastlings is an exhausting full-time job in its own right. Opening the bookstore would be an enormous task, and I was not prepared to attempt it with the kids in tow.

The interviewer suggested that I hold a book while I spoke—it gave me something to do with my hands, which was a small mercy—which provided an opportunity for some subtle advertising. I finished the piece by claiming that I'd rather wait and delay my opening until it was safer and easier to do so, which for me meant "when the schools go back." All the while, I was gripping a velvet-bound copy of Dickens' *Great Expectations* which I felt was appropriate given the topic of the interview. It was that or *100 Years of Solitude* by Gabriel Garcia Marquez which, although apt, felt a little dismal for the occasion.

The camera crew decided that my garage full of books was visually interesting enough to warrant some TV air time, and to my delight, they had a little drone with a camera designed just for these circumstances. The interview had been conducted outside because, even though in a few short weeks I would be having my grand re-opening, I *still* could not have guests standing within six feet of me in my untidy garage. Instead, CBC expertly flew the drone around inside, taking sweeping aerial shots of the mountains of book boxes. I was relieved that it neither crashed into something nor disappeared into L-space.

I was pleased that the footage from the garage looked so good on the television that evening, because it was not long after that things became even more crowded and ridiculous in there. Encouraged by the re-opening announcements, news from Sylvia regarding the imminent removal of her final bits and bobs, and an unexpectedly useful find on the local buy-and-sell group, Carl and I drove off to the north end of town to pick up twelve enormous shelving units. The seller had used them in his business, but had since closed down his shop, so the shelves were stored in his garage. He was keen to get rid of them as soon as possible and was asking a very reasonable price if they could be gone immediately. I wanted to purchase them quickly as well, as I was concerned someone else would snap them up if I didn't buy them straight away.

Best of all, I had received several texts from the landlady, Sylvia, saying that the building would be clear of her things, and ready to move in by the first week in June. This meant a July opening—coinciding neatly with the daycare expanding its capacity—was realistic. It gave me a clear month to get organised. I began by sending out a mass email to all my existing "surprise book" customers, and random people interested enough to have subscribed to my mailing list. I had a reassuring number of new subscribers following the CBC interview as well. I invited them to my July opening, and warned them of my capacity restrictions and social-distancing rules. The message was well-received, and there were many excited replies to my news along the lines of: *We can't wait to visit!* I finally felt a glimmer of confidence in my endeavour.

One Friday evening, Sylvia's brother called me, advising that he'd finished clearing and that we could begin moving in after the weekend. So, on Sunday, we picked up the shelving units, cramming them into our car and the truck my friend had so amiably brought over to help us with. On Monday, Carl and I packed up our new shelving finds and convoyed them to the building on his lunch break, ready to unload.

Just as we pulled into the parking space behind the building, we saw Sylvia arriving as well, and I waved at her excitedly. She did not wave back. In fact, she looked rather annoyed.

"You're not moving things in today, are you?" she asked crossly.

"Er, yes? Your brother called on Friday to say we could?"

"Well, he shouldn't have. It's not ready yet. I can't have anything touching the floors at the moment."

Dismayed, and more than a little angry myself, I tried to figure out what was going on this time. As her brother had confirmed on the phone, the space was indeed clear of all the family junk that had taken up the entire 1800 square feet of floor space. Multiple businesses had existed in the space over the decades, operated alternately by Sylvia, her brother, and even their parents before them. When I first saw the building, it was a shrine to antique office supplies. Broken stacking chairs lined the walls, and a colony of giant spider plants were stealthily annexing the back room. I spotted an elderly toilet with a pink fleece seat cover abandoned in one corner.

The front half of the space under the big window that I'd liked so much, was an ancient burial ground for photocopiers. It took a feat of naive and optimistic imagination to visualise it as a bookstore, or indeed, an empty building. By June though, Sylvia had at least read the photocopiers their last rites. Dozens of boxes of empty vodka bottles - apparently there from a hotel the family owned somewhere in rural Saskatchewan - had emerged from under the clutter and were now stacked neatly by the loading door ready for recycling. The junk was diminishing slightly each time I visited, which was very reassuring.

Seeing the place empty for the first time was overwhelming. It suddenly looked cavernous, to the point of being worrying. Five years earlier, I had rented a similar-sized, open-plan, and intimidatingly empty building for my coffee shop venture, and it turned out to be too big to use efficiently. Would the same prove true here? How would I ever fill it with books? My collection that had suffocated my garage for so long now seemed tiny and insignificant.

But it also looked so bright, sunny, and inviting with the yellow summer sun streaming in. A blank canvas, glowing with potential. The delays were crushing, I couldn't wait to get started.

However, getting started was not in the cards, according to Sylvia. The new floor, which was what had made the biggest improvement to the place's appearance, was tiled in a light grey pattern. Nothing exciting, but neutral and inoffensive, and considerably more attractive than the stained industrial brown carpet that had been there before. But the new floor tiles had to be waxed, and it was in this process where Sylvia's discontent lay. She had apparently had workmen in to wax the floor but was not impressed with the job they had done. Not for the first time, I felt like she was fixating on tiny details that did not matter in the grand scheme of things and was delaying things unnecessarily. She even said she was on the point of ripping it all up and starting again. She led me into the back room and tried to show me the cause of her frustration: tiny bubbles in the wax that had dried in place. At first, I could barely see what she meant. The bubbles were so small that they merged into the patterns on the tiles. They were only visible when the light hit them directly, and even then, it only spoiled the perfect shine; it made no material difference to the floor whatsoever. Sylvia, though, was adamant that it had to be redone and that to get it "to standard," it would take six coats on each area, and each coat needed 72 hours to dry completely before the next one could begin. As she was so unimpressed with the workmen's attempt, she resolved to do it herself, as well. This was going to be several weeks' work.

"You're looking at mid-July," Sylvia said, dispassionately. "I'm sorry, there's nothing I can do about it."

I found that hard to believe but managed to bite my tongue. Carl was also irate because now the new shelving units had to be squeezed into our garage as well as all the books, and we had no idea when we would ever be able to use the garage properly again. Worse still, we physically could not fit three of the twelve units in the garage, and we had no choice but to lodge them in the backyard. I bought large tarps to cover them with, but every time we had a dramatic prairie summer storm where the rain and hail threatened to soak the wood and warp my bookshelves, I became very anxious. If the volume of books I was storing was stressful enough for me to imagine them bending space and time, the addition of the shelves compounded the issue until I felt that there was a black hole in the backyard, and that I was teetering round the precarious ledge where at any minute I could fall into the eternal abyss.

That night I called my friend Rielle. We enjoy visiting in person more than talking on the phone, but meeting up was still not an option. Rielle used to work for me as a barista, so she had witnessed most of my bookstore planning, landlord dramas, and book buying antics before the pandemic. She had always cheered me on, and her loudmouth and blunt, dry humour made her the perfect candidate to cope with my frustrated ranting. I needed a dose of sweary optimism.

"It's bullshit delay after bullshit delay with that woman!" she said. "You should be as successful as possible, just to spite her." I couldn't have agreed more.

I reluctantly sent out another mailing list message with the bad news that, despite what I said last time, we would not in fact be opening next month. I sincerely hoped that people would not lose interest in the venture and assume I'd never open. I did receive a few replies with different versions of "Hang in there," but none were as succinct as Rielle's sympathies.

I avoided the building, and Sylvia over the next few weeks. I'd get anxious just thinking about it all. I did even start looking around for another building, but I couldn't find anything suitable or within budget. I kept telling myself not to worry. As I wasn't paying rent to Sylvia during these renovations, I assumed that she would probably like my rent money sooner rather than later and so it was in her interest to get things finished. Instead, I concentrated on my book deliveries and "pre-launch marketing," as my business mentor liked to call it.

Every time I passed the building on my bike deliveries, I would peer through the window (after first checking that Sylvia was not around, of course.) My glimpses did not inspire hope. Occasionally, I saw a mop bucket in the space, and it did seem to be being moved around, so there were some signs of life in there. I could not see any discernible difference in the floor though.

Most significantly, I once passed by the back of the building in the alley and saw not one, but two toilets sitting outside the back door along with a stainless-steel sink and faucet. The first toilet was the one with the pink fleece seat cover that had been in the junk pile. But the second one looked suspiciously like the one that had been in the downstairs—soon-to-be my shop's—bathroom. By sheer chance, Sylvia happened to step outside at that moment carrying a full garbage bag.

"Oh hello," she smiled, all friendly this time. "Coming to check up on it?" Caught, I nodded, dumbly. Sylvia explained, quite casually, that she'd decided to re-do the bathroom and kitchen area in the building, "to make it all nice for us." This included ripping out the toilet, basin, and the kitchen sink unit, eventually to be replaced. But how long would that take? My heart sank.

"The bathroom floor and the back room are all waxed now!" she told me.

And the main area?

No, that still needed another three coats, apparently.

Again, I was faced with no choice but to accept this, swallow my impatience, suppress the rising panic and readjust the tarps over the shelves in the yard.

In *The Picture of Dorian Gray*, Oscar Wilde writes: *The basis of optimism is sheer terror.* I felt this keenly when dealing with Sylvia. I had no choice but to stay optimistic about the bookstore's opening, because the alternative— never opening, never being able to break my lease with her, never being able to repay my loans, and being stuck with a garage filled to bursting with things I'd never use or sell—was too frightening to contemplate. Wilde's intensely creepy novella tells the story of Dorian Gray who pins his soul to an exceptionally attractive portrait of himself, to ensure he maintains his handsomeness forever. He then lives a life of sin and hedonism, yet never ages nor loses his looks. Meanwhile, locked away in a cupboard, his portrait rots away and grows uglier and uglier. At my most frustrated times, I began to wonder if Sylvia had done something similar with the bookstore building. The building was, after all, getting shinier and better looking, but I swear, somewhere in a darkened attic, there is a diorama of the bookstore, gradually getting dirtier and dirtier as Sylvia's soul decays below.

13
YOUTH

"My Mum is starting a bookstore with a coffee shop in it (we just call it 'the bookshop' though) and I had to go there every so often ALL SUMMER, but now that school has started, I don't have to. She gets help with her friend Rielle (I call her Real sometimes. She doesn't like that though.) She is nice but she swears A LOT." (From Milo's school journal, September 2020)

Rielle does swear a lot, but I do admit I gave her much to swear about that summer. Rielle sadly lost her job as a result of the lockdown, and, bored, available and strapped for cash as she was, I decided to employ her temporarily to help with *Operation Bookshelf*. Operation Bookshelf was such a monstrous undertaking that Milo was bribed—I mean, persuaded—to help too. Rielle and I tackled the flat-packed furniture, while Milo became an expert at putting books in alphabetical order.

My landlady Sylvia finally gave us the go-ahead to move into her building on Albert Street. Floor waxed to her satisfaction at last, she summoned me in to give me a key and help her mop the floor one final time. It really was shiny. I noticed, much to my despair, that she was filling the mop bucket by twisting the valve on bare pipes jutting out of the wall in the back room. There was still no sink or real tap. Sylvia put her finger over the jet of water to increase the pressure and fill the bucket faster. As I crouched to help her, the cold water squirted straight in my face. Shocked, I shrieked, but tried to laugh it off. Sylvia smiled but did not seem surprised. I could swear it was deliberate.

Now, to finally turn an empty shell of a building into a cosy bookstore— in two weeks. It was already mid-August, and it was impossibly hot. Sylvia had vacated and was not answering her phone, so I wasn't able to ask about the air conditioning. I coerced my daughter Theia into returning to daycare, which she was happy to do as soon as she realised she was allowed to play in their sprinkler. Milo, on the other hand, had to accompany me to work. He cycled over to the building every day. Faced with the prospect of physical exercise *and* having to hang out with Mum over his summer break, he could only be consoled with a daily giant Slurpee from the convenience store opposite my new shop. A couple of Milo's friends came by to "help," or at least distract and entertain him for a while, and soon we were replacing books in the boxes with empty Slurpee cups and popsicle wrappers.

Rielle still drank bucketsful of coffee, even in 30°C heat, so the coffee bar was the first thing to be set up, negating the need to buy coffee as well as the neon sodas favoured by the kids. All this was done without any running water in the space; the sink was gone, and Sylvia had not replaced the toilet either. Given the time constraints, I just had to accept the current situation and trust that the final renovations would be done soon. After waiting so long to move in, and the scale of Operation Bookshelf being so intimidating, a little thing like having running water in my new coffee bar suddenly dropped down the priority list.

I had planned a seating area to surround the coffee bar and this I thought we could make a start on, drama-free. I had bought a dozen chairs and three large tables—all flat packed—to form a small cafe. To this day, the chairs are the bane of my existence. Each one has twelve bolts holding the seat to the legs—which sit at perverse angles to the seat itself. Each bolt must be screwed in with a specialised wrench, while you are positioned upside down while jabbing yourself in the stomach with the legs. Rielle and I dealt with these, but it took us the best part of a week to complete them all. Even now, I have to go around and tighten up each bolt once a month as they seem to loosen by themselves, just to spite me.

Then came the physically demanding task of hauling the shelving units into place and stacking them on top of each other. It was such a relief to get them out of our backyard, and Carl gleefully drove them over on his lunch breaks, two at a time. He helped Rielle and I wrestle them into the shop and put them into position—we were eternally grateful. Sylvia had not, in fact, cleared everything out of the building as promised, but had left the floor polisher machine she'd been using, a pile of spare baseboard planks, and an old, but exceedingly heavy countertop by the door to my leased space. It proved exceedingly tricky to lift our furniture around it. Sylvia returned once and actually shouted at me as if I were a naughty child because moving a shelf around her mess had scuffed the precious wax on the floor. Pointing out that this was the whole point of waxing the floor in the first place, to protect it, did nothing to alleviate her anger.

Rielle is a couple of years older than me, but by the end of that first week we both were feeling achy and decrepit, having aged at least a decade inside a few days of Do-It-Yourself renovations.

It was around this point that I received an email from a woman named Astrid, and I confess, I very nearly ignored it. Astrid was both asking for a job and wanting me to take her two poetry books on consignment. Up to my waist in book boxes, exhausted from the DIY, and worrying myself into a frenzy at the prospect of sending both children back to full-time school in a pandemic, I was not really paying much attention to the numerous messages from keen local writers. Or the many, many people who were looking for work after the lockdown and who shared my romantic "magical-book-haven" fantasy. I did worry that I had more people wanting to be booksellers than people wanting to be book buyers.

But Astrid was different. And tenacious. And supremely confident. Astrid made sure to follow up her first email with a resume, and then a request to meet. I invited her for the grand tour—of the empty building and Milo's nest of Slurpee garbage, thinking it might be enough to put her off. It was not that easy. On first impressions, Astrid was not as confident in person as she sounded via email, but I can't really blame her for that as she walked into chaos. Milo hid, immersed in headphones. Rielle and Astrid eyed each other nervously and I talked too much to mask the awkwardness. I did not have a lot of confidence in my own endeavour at that point.

Astrid, though, was not to be dissuaded by mere construction mess. I was grateful for her enthusiasm, as I was also beginning to realise the limits of what could be achieved by one person and a few coerced helpers. I was going to need proper staff, sooner or later; however, I didn't have a clear idea in my head of who I wanted to work with. I had deliberately chosen not to find a business partner for this venture because I neither wanted to work with friends for fear of wrecking valued relationships, nor look for a stranger who would, I assumed, need me to explain my vision coherently and require proof that I wasn't completely mad. It was much easier, to my mind at least, to go it alone. But I would need people to *work* for me, eventually. Sensible, reliable people who could work with little supervision. People who I could trust to just get on with things. I have had more than my fair share of terrible bosses—the micromanagers, the bullies, the traditionalists threatened by anything new, and the "seagulls" (the type who fly in suddenly, make a lot of noise and figuratively poop over everything, then fly off again). Those people were largely responsible for my entrepreneurial tendencies, and I was absolutely determined that I would never inflict that type of leadership on anyone else.

Astrid returned soon after the initial meeting, this time with the excuse of dropping off copies of her two poetry books for me to stock. We talked some more—about books, of course—and I was keen to see if Astrid would "fit." Would we get on okay? Would she love the bookshop even if it turned out to be as eccentric as my projects inevitably are? She reads a great deal—but not the sorts of books I would normally pick up. As a sort of interview question or test for potential employees, I ask them to sell me their favourite book. Astrid's was *Chasers of the Light*, a poetry book by Tyler Knott Gregson, one I had never heard of but that she described as "life-changing." Tyler Knott Gregson began the book by typing a brief, impromptu poem on an antique typewriter he'd found. The analog typewriter prevents the poet from editing the work in any way once typed, producing a raw but highly authentic poem. In my head, I drew parallels to my own situation. I had to develop the confidence to just *begin* this business, just as Knott Gregson had started typing. The business would be raw and messy and rough around the edges at first, but I hoped we'd create something beautiful with it.

Astrid had bright orange hair that not only clashed horribly with my cherry-red dye, but also with the vibrant green velvet couch that Rielle and I had just dragged into place under the window. I was also a little worried by her age; not that I had anything against creative types in their twenties, I just knew that I would be delegating considerable responsibilities to anyone I hired, and I wanted someone who would embrace that easily, someone perhaps with a bit of experience. Despite these concerns, I began to feel more and more that Astrid would fit in brilliantly. I needed someone who actually read and understood poetry, but who cared about Instagram too.

Her next email made the decision easier. I already thought I could see a lot of myself in Astrid, or at least, a lot of my younger self, but she was still capable of surprising me. Her third email had "Proposition for you!" in the subject line. I hoped it was in the business sense. Having seen the scope of Operation Bookshelf and my desire to get the place open as soon as possible, Astrid was offering to work for free, helping to set up the shop and build shelves, in exchange for being put "top of the highering list" for my potential staff. That way, she argued, she'd already know the layout of the store and be familiar with the stock before we opened. That was something I knew I would never have had the confidence to do myself when I was younger. I was so impressed by her audacity that I could overlook the spelling error.

For the record, she was already at the top of my hiring list, mainly because she was the only one who had forced me to even think about employing people—although I don't think I've ever admitted that to her. I invited her in again the next day and got her to screw together yet another flat-packed bookshelf. She managed it, then arranged her poetry books on it, proudly. One of them, amusingly, is called *Youth*. Astrid's bookshelf remains the wobbliest one in the store, but nevertheless, I sent her home that evening with a job offer letter.

Now a team of four-plus-Carl, within two weeks we managed to get the place furnished, stocked, and looking like a bookstore. My vague attempts at Instagram and Facebook promotions took off, and we began to be noticed by local traditional media as well. It was exciting for all of us. Milo and Theia went back to school in September; Milo extremely reluctantly after six months off, Theia bouncing along in excitement at starting Kindergarten, and me both proud and paranoid. Clad in masks and with copious amounts of hand sanitiser in their backpacks, we apprehensively approached the school. The playground was half-empty— the school had introduced a "staggered start" to avoid having 450 snotty-nosed, potentially infectious children in one space at one time. Parents were discouraged from hanging around too long and were not allowed to even enter the playground. Milo's class was called in first, leaving Theia and I hovering behind the wire fence. Theia clung to my knee until her new teacher appeared and expertly herded her class away, unable to briefly greet the parents, or even smile at us from behind her mask. I went home and cried.

But then, it was time to start working on my "soft opening," and that was a much more cheerful, positive thing to worry about. Carl had been told to return to his office (a command he resented intensely, having become quite comfortable in the work-from-home lifestyle). Being on my own again after "sheltering in place" with my family for twenty-four long weeks felt beyond strange. I missed the kids terribly, despite my relief at not having to entertain them all day, every day. The house was eerily quiet, and soon I found myself pedalling as quickly as possible to the bookstore after dropping the kids at school, just to avoid the emptiness and loneliness. I craved people, crowds, and company.

Now, with my focus on re-entering the business community at full force, how was I to get the whole of Regina to visit my new business? I turned again to my mailing list and announced that the official opening day would be September 12th, but that people were welcome to come visit for a few days before that to check the place out. I posted similar announcements on social media and received an amazing response, and for those first few days, it felt as though the whole city was as excited as I was to see my new entrepreneurial adventure come to life.

At the time, Astrid was still working at another job, and couldn't work weekends at The Penny University. During my soft opening days when people were wandering in purely out of curiosity, I met Ian when he dropped by the shop, pushing his tiny, sweet baby daughter in a stroller. Ian is an avid reader who came in to inquire about jobs. In his twenties and a new stay-home dad, he was after a very part-time job to get him out the house and provide a bit of extra cash. But unlike every other applicant, he had actually worked in an independent bookstore before. He did a very convincing job of selling me *Buttermilk Graffiti* by Edward Lee, which is part cookbook, part memoir, part social commentary. I am a big fan of foodie-anthropology, but this was not a title I'd come across before, and it pleased me that I now had two potential booksellers with reading tastes quite different to my own. This would definitely help me curate the stock. Learning about *Buttermilk Graffiti* had also made me hungry. As soon as Ian left, I experienced an uncontrollable urge to go eat a giant bowl of kimchi noodles. I sent him a job offer via email as soon as I had finished stuffing my face.

Official opening day arrived. I want to say it was a gloriously sunny, warm day, but I honestly can't remember what the weather was doing. Ian was to start the following week, and in all the chaos of last-minute preparations, I'd somehow convinced myself that I could manage the opening day at the store all by myself. I was 37 years old and this was my *fifth* "opening day" experience with various business ventures since 2009. I had, quite literally, written a book about how *not* to do it. But, it took a 22-year-old who had only met me a week earlier to point out that maybe trying to cope alone wasn't the best idea. Astrid had taken it upon herself to book a day off from her other job and volunteered to join me for the opening. I was gushingly grateful.

Astrid was right—of course it would have been far too much for one person to handle. The two of us were rushed off our feet with customers for eight hours straight. I made the coffees as I hadn't yet trained Astrid to do so, and she bravely rang up books on my untested new Point of Sale system. Even so, we were nearly overwhelmed. There were many teething issues— we had no barcode scanner, meaning that Astrid had to type in at least the beginning of each title sold so that our computer could find it, which was very time consuming. Our internet connection was not yet hooked up and we were entirely reliant on mobile data which further slowed the rate of sales being rung through. Amusingly, the debit card reader and the music ran off the same Bluetooth connection, and so the music paused every time someone paid for something! Thankfully, our customers were understanding that day and patient with us learning as we went.

Ian and his wife popped in with their daughter tucked into the stroller, but the place proved too crowded for an indignant eight-month-old and her Covid-19-anxious parents, and they didn't stay long. Carl brought our kids in, but I barely got to say hello to them either.

People kept coming in. Friends, vague acquaintances, a newly elected member of the school board, the former manager from Astrid's other job. Several people who I knew worked for CBC. Someone I had met a handful of times at various artistic endeavours in Regina brought her friend in to introduce me to him. The friend turned out to be none other than Tristan Derocher, the young man from La Ronge who had walked 635 km to Regina to raise awareness about Indigenous suicide. He was on a hunger strike until the government agreed to meet him to talk, and on that day, he looked thin, pale, and exhausted. I was truly honoured that he had made it in to see us, and I felt terrible that I had no time for us to have a proper conversation.

But still they came; not just to browse either—but to buy armfuls and armfuls of beautiful new books. For a panicked moment, I thought we wouldn't have enough left on the shelves for when Day 2 arrived. Astrid joked that we should have shopping carts. There were so many compliments about the store, about our range of books, about how brave I was for even attempting this. As the tiredness set in, I started to worry that we'd inadvertently created a "super spreader" event, with too many people in a small space, all breathing germs on my beloved books. We'd done everything we could—spaced everything out with the regulation six-foot gaps between them, insisted that each and every person used the sanitizer before touching the books, didn't allow anyone to drink their coffee in the shop. I had coughed experimentally—no sore throat. I opened a hardback book and sniffed at the pages. It smelled of New Book (not that delicious musty-vanilla fragrance of old books—sadly that smell needs time to develop); my olfactory nerves were still intact. So far, so good, I thought. My paranoia was due entirely to nervous exhaustion, not Covid-19.

We took in the entire month's rent in sales that day. Beyond even my wildest hopes of what could be achieved in eight hours. It truly felt as though I'd tapped into the zeitgeist, that this was exactly what was wanted, what was needed in this place and at this time. It was incredibly encouraging. Now all I had to do was do it all again the next day.

I sent Astrid home with a couple of free books and a million thank yous, knowing full well I could not have survived without her. Chatting with the kids over dinner that night, I realised that Astrid is closer to Milo's age than mine. "Hah, you're old!" he said, pointing at me. I was too exhausted to disagree.

14
PENNIES AND WOLF WOMEN

For many people, I am now "Penny." Admittedly, *The Penny University* is not an obvious name for a bookshop, and so it is a logical assumption that the owner may be called Penny. I am not opposed to this idea, and rarely correct people.

The identity of someone—or something—called Penny at the bookstore is further confirmed by the fact that our inventory software can now send out messages to customers by itself, and it signs itself off with the abbreviation, *Penny U*. I am minorly concerned that the laptop will one day gain sentience and that "Penny" will emerge, pixelated and green, intent on ridding the world of the scourge of humanity (or at least, those of us who say "me either" or "have you got that new one by Thingy, with the red cover?") But for now, we seem to be safe enough with my alter-ego.

Pennies—the discontinued copper coin—do play an important role in operations, however. During the lockdown summer of 2020, while I was waiting impatiently to open the store, I made all sorts of attempts at craftiness using pennies. Some were more successful than others.

Years before, a friend had moved from Regina to Victoria, BC and had bestowed on us the treasures that couldn't travel with him. One of those treasures was a margarine tub full of pennies. Why on earth I thought to keep these, I do not know, as it was long after Canada ceased their use as currency. I think I might have intended to teach Milo to gamble with them just as my mum taught me at a similar age; playing blackjack is an excellent way of teaching quick mental arithmetic.

After the schools closed in March, my supply of ideas for educational activities dried up astonishingly quickly. I had high hopes for my success as a home-based teacher! I did not consider myself inexperienced. After all, while in Latin America, I taught English to children of a similar age to Theia. While employed at the Saskatchewan Science Centre, had I not spent two years entertaining children and adults with scientific wonders? Even at university, I tutored undergrads. But homeschooling my own kids in a pandemic? Fat chance! My two knew the exact limits of my patience, knew what they could get away with, and most importantly knew just how far they could push a situation before it affected their father's ability to work in peace—the man who was also confined to the house trying to actually earn a living and keep us all fed. My limit was simple: I'd pursue the activity only until it interrupted Carl's work.

Penny crafting was not my best idea. The children and I watched many Pinterest videos on gluing pennies around balloons to make pretty copper bowls. This was an unmitigated disaster, as four-year-olds and balloons *and* glue are never a good combination. I did make some penny coasters for the store, using old book pages to back them with, but that was a private evening endeavour because it required a hot glue gun. Gambling with pennies was popular, right up until Milo won and started gloating. Theia threw things in retaliation and Carl yelled at them. It was a very long summer.

Eventually, I hit on the idea of the surprise book subscription deliveries. This ticked many useful boxes. It helped thin out the books I'd already amassed in the garage in anticipation of opening, the kids could help prepare the packages, it would get me out of the house and cycling, *and* it involved pennies.

My subscription book packages eventually became so popular that I employed Milo to help me pack them. Each month, I wrapped the specially chosen book in brown paper, poured sealing wax on it and stuck a shiny penny in the wax, while Milo packed the coffee and other goodies in big manila envelopes. Theia then accompanied me biking around the city to deliver them.

The pennies I had in the margarine tub were grubby, tarnished and slightly smelly, and did not make for attractive decoration on my book packages. So, we employed *science!* Milo, Theia and I experimented with how to clean the copper coins, using whatever we could find in the kitchen. Vinegar worked, and white vinegar was better than malt. Nail polish remover just stank. Soapy water had little effect on the tarnish, but the detergent did eradicate the smell. Bleach dulled them, but Coca-Cola worked best of all. Acids and alkalis! Testing hypotheses! Education!

Armed with our newly cleaned bright pennies, I started a subscription package production line, wrapping the books, melting sealing wax and then pressing a penny into it. Melting the sealing wax was not the cutesy, romantic process that I thought it to be. I had purchased little blobs of deep red wax and the kit came with a spoon and a tiny tea-light candle. You heated the metal spoon over the candle and the wax blob melted inside the bowl of the spoon. The little tea-light was soon used up however, and so I switched to a cigarette lighter thus making it look even more like we were cooking heroin.

I should clarify that I have never in my life cooked drugs or even seen anyone doing so. As a teenager, I was deeply disturbed by the graphic descriptions of heroin use in Irvine Welsh's book *Trainspotting*. Other than the small knowledge I gained from Welsh's words and images, I am naive and clueless. That book alone is more powerful than any school-safe "don't do drugs, kids" campaign. As an adult, however, and living a hugely privileged life, I have not had cause to give the topic much thought. That was until we were introduced to a local author named Beatrice Wolfe.

Beatrice, known as the "Wolf Woman" after her book of the same name, bravely did a reading at the bookstore as part of a reading series with the Saskatchewan Book Awards. I knew she was an Indigenous woman from the Muskowekwan First Nation in Saskatchewan, and a sexual assault survivor who had written a memoir. But nothing really prepared me for her reading.

"Harrowing" is not a word I've ever had much reason to use before, but the word is not severe enough in this context. *Wolf Woman* is an incredible story of tragedy, betrayal, bravery and determination. As she read to a small audience (restricted by the Covid-19 capacity limits at the time), I filmed her for a Facebook Live event. Watching the video, you can clearly tell when my hands started shaking while holding the camera. I genuinely teared up.

I lay awake for a long time that night as I could not get her story out of my head. At fourteen years old, she had escaped from her abusive school and uncaring adoptive mother with the help of an older girl who had "family" outside the school and somewhere to run to. The family turned out to be a bunch of addicts in a squat house. Beatrice was injected with heroin, not knowing what it was or what it would do to her. She was then raped while only semi-conscious. The events of this single night set her on a path to addiction, trauma, and homelessness that lasted years.

The cruelty and betrayal in this book is unfathomable, and for me, meeting this striking, strong and yet humble woman, now sober and smiling in my shop, was simply incredible. She left that small audience stunned and reeling. Knowing she has survived and is forging a happy, successful life for herself now did little to stop me replaying her words in my head that night, but it is perhaps the most poignant source of hope that I have yet come across.

As we clapped for her after her reading, Beatrice thanked "Penny" for hosting her, and admired the wax and penny seals on the pile of subscription books on the counter. "Those are pretty," she said. "I've not seen real seals like that before, only in old movies."

15
RENTING FROM THE MAFIA BOSS

Apparently, per capita, Regina is the crime-capital of Canada. Or at least, it vies for that title with Thunder Bay and Winnipeg. This used to amuse me a great deal. Coming from the UK, the city is a leafy utopia in comparison. In my former hometown of Darlington, you would never see the police putting out reminders for people to lock their car doors to prevent theft. Anything not locked up—and sometimes even things that were—would disappear instantly. As we began the emigration process and spent an experimental few weeks in Regina before moving over officially, our house in Darlington was broken into and trashed. Amongst other things, they took our TV and Xbox, Carl's guitar, and the jewellery my Nan had bought me for my wedding. (In many ways the burglars did us a favour, as we could not have taken the electronics with us to Canada as we would need voltage transformers to get them to work. At least this way, we were paid insurance money, which was more useful at the time than attempting to sell off our used electronics before moving.) But the whole experience scarred us—it was a horrible violation, and something that only served to strengthen our resolve to leave and never go back.

I have had a bicycle or two stolen in Regina —as has pretty much everyone I know. Bike theft is a big problem and hugely frustrating as it is yet another barrier preventing people from embracing cycling in this city. But for the most part, the crime in Regina is opportunistic theft, it is rarely violent. Stabbings and murders do happen here, but they are rare phenomenon that receive intense news coverage. In Darlington, someone was stabbed in our local pub, and died later that night in hospital. The pub reluctantly closed for a few hours, but then re-opened in time for the evening rush, still with police tape around the door. I know this because I happened to walk past when the flashing police lights were still outside. The incident did not even make the local news.

Coming from such a place has made Regina seem positively glorious in comparison, and I am admittedly complacent about crime here. It was somewhat of a surprise then, when we found ourselves witnessing some shady dealings at the Albert Street bookstore building. Of course, the bookstore was home to a great many creative types with vivid imaginations. Astrid, Ian and I include ourselves in that category. As such, the bookstore was the perfect place to invent dramatic backstories to the odd instances of suspicious activity, and it turned out that Sylvia the landlady had plenty of secrets that lent themselves nicely to abundant storytelling.

Before leasing the space for the store, I researched the owners as best I could. I have been burned by too many landlords, so I was cautious. I knew that Sylvia's family were very well off, owned multiple properties and had operated several businesses in Saskatchewan. At the time, Sylvia appeared to be running some sort of financial advisory service, from her office above the bookstore. I knew she sat up there by herself most weekdays, and I heard the phone ring fairly frequently, but I never saw a single person go into or come out of her office.

The situation became even more intriguing. First, we had a call from a local distillery. I knew of them from the Regina business groups, and at first thought they were calling just to say hello as we opened up nearby. But no, they were calling because they thought I was Sylvia, and wanted to ask whether I/she was still selling "the still." So, Sylvia apparently had a distilling operation going on somewhere. Seems unusual for a financial advisor. Unsure whether this was a legal, licensed venture or not, I politely gave the guy the correct phone number for Sylvia and didn't tell her that I'd heard the request.

After we had been open for two weeks, the big Penny University sign was installed on the side of the building. It was six foot high, positioned about 15 feet in the air above the sidewalk—and I was exceedingly proud of it. Paying for it proved to be a further interesting escapade. It was not that I was short of money; I had budgeted accordingly, asked for a quote, and was fully expecting to receive a bill. The company I had hired to do the work came from a recommendation from Sylvia, and as I know nothing about sign making, I took her advice. I received the invoice, paid it, admired my sign, and assumed that was the end of the matter.

A couple of months later, Sylvia sent me a terse email asking when she could expect payment for the sign! I was stunned. I told her, not that it was any of her business, but that I'd paid it several weeks ago. I even showed her the receipt. She was furious, and for the life of me I could not figure out why. Eventually she explained, angrily, that the sign guy owed her money. She had recommended I get the sign done by him, so that I could then give *her* the money which would settle his debt to her. Neither Sylvia nor my sign maker had explained this unspoken agreement to me at the time, and it is certainly not something I would have guessed at by myself. The invoice was addressed to me from the sign company, so I paid it directly to them, unaware that Sylvia had any interest in the transaction. I am glad they didn't explain it; I did not want to get involved with any of her odd financial dealings.

The Godfather movie, released in 1972, is an adaptation of the Puzo novel of the same name. The Godfather Part II, released in 1974, also adapts elements from the first novel, but the story of The Godfather Part III was written entirely for the movie. This iconic trilogy seems to have epitomised the genre, as it is now referenced, parodied and satirised in many different media forms, from Disney's Zootopia movie, The Sopranos TV show, and comic references in cartoons like The Simpsons, Family Guy and South Park. More obscurely, in 1997, Welsh indie band Catatonia released a single called *I am the Mob* with several Godfather references in the lyrics and in 2013, famous lines from the movie were used in a pizza advert that promised the company would "make you a pizza you can't refuse." The movies, and indirectly, the original novel still permeate pop culture some fifty years after the movies' releases.

I have not read many mafia novels, but the influence of *The Godfather* is so prevalent that I feel I still should have seen what was happening around us. It wasn't long before my mental image of Sylvia had gone from Mad Old Woman In The Attic to Godmother and mafia boss, based on my limited knowledge of Mario Puzo's novel. We imagined her family—the miserly father, unnervingly quiet mother observing everything, the brother acting as the Fixer—populating this narrative neatly. Our collective and overactive imaginations were running wild, and after the days when I'd had unpleasant interactions with Sylvia, I went to bed expecting to wake up in the morning next to a horse's head.

There is a point in most mafia novels, and in almost all mafia movies, where the innocent protagonist mistakenly gets involved with something he shouldn't, beyond any hope of redemption. The readers know what's coming, can see the fatal error and are left yelling at the book, "Noooo! Don't do that!" But of course, the character does, and the consequences are severe. Secret stills and dodgy deals with sign companies aside, the final *dramatic Point Of No Return* in our business relationship came when three men, whom I can only describe as Goons, marched into my bookstore.

They immediately looked like Trouble. I've worked in pubs and bars long enough to know what Trouble generally looks like, but I felt Bookstore Trouble would be better attired, with suits and clipboards from some sort of literary inspection agency. These three were just tough-looking workmen, in cargo pants and loose button-down shirts. And steel-toed boots, I noticed. I felt very grateful that my friend James was in the store at the time. James is a sweet-natured nerd with a bad back, but on first impression is a big-framed, six-foot-tall older man with presence and a deep voice. I am hardly frail and timid myself, but having him around gave me a confidence boost.

"You the owner?" the tallest Goon asked.

Stupidly I said, "Yes," thinking of my store.

"She owns the business," James interjected. "Are you looking for the building owner? Because she's probably upstairs." One of them nodded, and they all moved towards the back of the room.

Sylvia still had a large quantity of her own furniture and belongings lodged in an alcove at the back of the bookstore. Most of it was too heavy to move by myself—a solid oak desk, a couch with a heavy wooden frame, and an enormous steel press (the sort used for clamping and cutting large stacks of paper.) It still had a frighteningly large steel blade in it. I had no idea where it came from or what Sylvia's family were doing with it— just one more thing that went utterly unexplained. So unexpected was its existence in my store that I'd decided to view it as a curiosity, a strange phenomenon unique to the space. I had long since given up hope that Sylvia might move it out of my shop as promised.

It was this press that the Goons were interested in. "Is she in?" the head Goon asked, tilting his head to mean "upstairs." I made a pretence of calling up the stairs for Sylvia, but knew she wasn't in the building that day. Perhaps deliberately.

"Do you want me to give her a message?" I ventured.

"Yeah. Tell her she needs to talk to me. I'm Daryl. She owes me money, and if I don't see it soon, we're gonna come back here and take this press. I don't wanna mess up your shop here, but I need what's owed. You can tell her that."

I tried to seem calm and unfazed. "Can I get your phone number, so she can call you?" I think this rattled him somewhat—a woman asking for his phone number in a brisk and business-like manner probably was at least a little unexpected, but he let me write it down, and eventually, with threatening glances around the shop, all three of them finally left.

"Wow," said James, exhaling slowly. "Are you okay? What the hell was that all about?"

I told him I had no idea. Above the phone number, which I'd scrawled on a bright orange post-it note, I carefully printed: *DARYL - wtf?!* Then I marched upstairs and stuck it on Sylvia's door. I'd informed her. Duty done.

Sylvia never mentioned the incident, although the post-it note did vanish quickly. To this day, I do not know if she paid up, or if she got her Family to fix the situation for her. Either way, the press still did not move from the back of the shop. I took to dusting it occasionally, just in case. I realised that this must have been my own point of no return. I was now inextricably entangled with Sylvia and what can only be called her *organised crime network*. Idly, I considered whether I could fake my own death to get out of the lease, but I'd have too many "assets" in the form of books to sneak out of the building in secret and I dare not confront her either. The only course of action was to keep my head down, turn a blind eye to all her indiscretions and hope for the best.

16
NOT COLONISING THE MOON

We had been open for a couple of months and were beginning to stock up for the anticipated Christmas rush, when my cousin Oliver called me at the bookstore. As Oliver has a history of depression and mental illness, and calls so rarely, I immediately panicked and assumed he must be in trouble. I snatched the phone up, alarmed.

"Are you ok? What's up?"

"Oh nothing. Just bored. Thought I'd annoy you."

"I appreciate the thought, but I'm in the shop now. I only answered because I assumed you were dying or something. Can I call you back later? I've got customers."

"What, actual humans? With real money?"

I should point out here that I am very fond of my cousin. I also delight in teasing him and proving him wrong. We are equally stubborn and proud, and as a result, our inconsequential arguments can last days. It's wonderful. This time, however, I had made him entirely incredulous.

I called Oliver back later and, I admit, I did boast a little. I felt I was justified. Our opening day was spectacular and the rest of the first month had been extraordinary as well. It had lulled a bit in October, but as soon as Remembrance Day had passed, most Reginans started Christmas shopping in earnest. This would be a lucrative Christmas for retail. Travelling was still banned, as was gathering in groups larger than six, which put paid to most people's plans for the holidays. Instead, they overcompensated with gifts, and we were extremely busy in the bookstore.

The fact that Oliver was surprised that I had customers gave me a great opportunity for some gentle teasing and bragging.

"We took $7,220 last week."

"Fuckinell, and I was a naysayer."

"I never expected any different from you."

"I had no idea people still wanted books!"

"Everyone seems so excited. It's been lovely."

"Where do you get books from? How do you know which ones people want? What the hell is a book anyway?" (Sarcasm runs strong in my family.)

"The first person who came in on Friday said, 'I haven't bought books in six months, this is amazing!' and spent $147 in one go. I get them from big book distributors—a few in Canada, and a massive company in the US—and from publishers' reps. I got a little bit of everything in to interest people, and then took requests from them."

"Well now I have more questions than answers! 'A bit of everything' and you'd have a library! And requests?! Why do people request books from a bookstore when they could just get it delivered? My brain hurts!"

"Why get one book delivered when you can browse hundreds of them?" I retorted.

I did struggle to respond to that one, however. I think by November 2020, people were just plain sick of online shopping and deliveries. Given the pandemic, I had expected it to be much harder to tempt people from their homes and out into the snow to come browse books, but most seemed to regard the outing as an exotic luxury.

"I do requests because I can't possibly stock everything ever published, so people just tell me what they want and I order it in for them. But they usually get distracted in the store when requesting things and buy other books too. I understand the need to shop online, especially at the moment, but you can't really browse on Amazon, you have to know what you're looking for. In a real store, you can have a proper look through things and find stuff you've never heard of."

"But if I want to know something, I just look it up on the internet. Information books might be more convenient, perhaps."

"I don't really do those because I have no idea what's useful in terms of how-to books. I just stock *Things That Might Be Interesting*. Anyway, you can't read novels online. Well, you can, but it's not enjoyable."

"But you can order them to your door if you've read a good review. It's the requests thing that confuses me the most. If someone knows what they want it just seems like a no-brainer to get it online."

"But sociability?" I ask. "The need to get out the house ..." I continued, "I know you don't do *people*—" (this is an understatement) "so how about immediacy? Choose a book, pay for it and it's in your hand instantly. Or maybe a desire to support small local businesses rather than lining Jeff Bezos's pockets further?"

There is a pause and I know I am losing him. "Is it me that's weird?" he asks, redundantly.

"Well, obviously." This isn't a video call, but I can already feel his death-stare.

"Anyway," he says, malevolence abated. "All my cynicism needs to be expunged, you've won the business game, so congrats!"

"Thank you. Maybe ask me again in January when it's minus eleven billion and no one goes out shopping, and I might start agreeing with you."

People did love ordering from us, and at first, we enjoyed finding the interesting and obscure things people asked for. Of course, there were a few jokers—the 3D versions of online trolls. One guy with spiky blue hair under an ageing grey sun visor, overheard me tell someone that we could usually order in "anything," and so proceeded to ask me to order him a piano. Not a book of sheet music for pianos (which I would have struggled with anyway); no, he wanted me to order an actual piano. I assumed this was a joke and told him I had to restrict the orders to books only, but not long after, he returned to the store, requesting, "The Greatest Book Ever Written!" I hazarded a few guesses—*Hitchhiker's Guide to the Galaxy*, maybe? *The Oxford English Dictionary*? Or *How to Avoid Large Ships* by John W. Trimmer? No, he wanted an electronic copy of the *Bible!* Not an eBook; apparently you can buy devices like Kindle or Kobo readers that only contain the text of the Bible. In case storing other eBooks on it is blasphemous, I suppose. Maybe they have consecrated memory cards in them. Either way, this was also not available through my regular book distributors, so it was another polite "No" from us. Obviously, this made us heathens or infidels, and after a rather rude exchange, the man left and has fortunately never returned. I hope he found his piano and digital Bible elsewhere. But I doubt it.

Despite my boasting to Oliver, the orders in the shop were getting overwhelming, especially when we had Christmas as a deadline to get things in. We found ourselves competing with huge, multi-branch companies for that year's Christmas bestsellers, and as a new shop with no credit history with the distributors, we discovered we were often at the bottom of the heap when it came to distributing books in short supply. I was proud that we managed to get Obama's *A Promised Land* on the day it was released, but I underestimated the demand for the 750-page, $55 hardback from the former president and we sold out straight away. The second batch did not arrive quite so quickly and we started to panic. It was very rewarding seeing people so pleased with their purchases when they did finally arrive.

A less successful purchase was a box of *Shuggie Bain* by Douglas Stuart. This book won the Booker prize and was suddenly incredibly popular— right after I had done all my Christmas ordering. I confess, I had never heard of the book prior to its win and had not ordered in advance. We had over a dozen requests for the grim tale of poverty and alcoholism set in 1980s Glasgow, all for Christmas gifts, and none of the distributors had any left to sell me.

An older gentleman wanted to purchase *Shuggie Bain*. Unfortunately, he did not use email and only left a landline phone number with us, which at the time we had patiently copied into our handwritten order ledger. Every day for well over a month, before and after Christmas, he shuffled into the shop to ask after his book. Every day we told him, no, sorry, we would call as soon as it arrived. After Christmas he came in less frequently, until eventually he gave up on us.

In February 2021, a mysterious box arrived from one of our bigger distributors. I assessed the size, and realised that it couldn't be the order I'd placed the previous week. Yippee! I do like surprise packages, particularly when they are books. Astrid and I opened the box. A dozen copies of *Shuggie Bain* greeted us. Finally! I assigned Astrid the unenviable task of calling people to say that the book they'd requested two months ago was now available, while I conveyed the same message via email. Half the people who'd requested it had given up the wait and had bought it at Indigo or online, but they had the courtesy to sound apologetic about that.

Last on our list was the elderly gentleman who had visited so patiently. Astrid dialled the number. *"Baaarp. Baaaarp. Baaaarp. This number is not in service. Please check the number and try again."* I tried myself, in case she had typed the number wrong. *"This number is not in service. Please check and try again.*" All that waiting, and we couldn't contact him! We were devastated. The gentleman has never been seen again. To date, we still have four copies of *Shuggie Bain* on the shelf from that original shipment. They remain there stubbornly, an unwelcome monument to a brief zeitgeist and missed opportunity.

We also had a few nice "wins." One man, especially wary of Covid-19, wanted books with a contact-less delivery. I emailed him an invoice, and he paid within minutes. Fortunately, he was after a title that we had on the shelves already; the latest Hilary Mantel book. I looked at the delivery address—right behind my house. When Astrid arrived for the afternoon shift, I took the book home with me, and put it in his mailbox as I walked to the daycare to pick Theia up. When I got home again, there was a 5-star review waiting for me on the store's Facebook page: *Ordered this on my lunch break today. On my doorstep by 4 p.m. Beat that, Amazon!*

Boosted by this feedback, we made ourselves a new chalkboard outside the shop: *This holiday season, buy books from people who want to sell you books, not people who want to colonise the moon.*

The day after my chat with the incredulous Oliver, we were sent another book request via email. It was from Mattie in Moose Jaw and ironically, it is one that would require me to mail the book out—I can't compete with Amazon's shipping times here. Mattie used to support my coffee shop in times past, and once introduced me to someone as "that strange Brit who brings caffeine." Whereas I am familiar with his humour, the subject line of his email amused me no end:

"BOOK ORDER" it read "because Eff Amazon!!"

17
INTOXICATING SPACES

As the season's second dose of heavy snow fell and the temperature dipped towards -30°C, I cycled downtown. The curb was already being used as a snow dump, so I avoided the main road and the truck drivers who would scream obscenities when I dared exist in the center of the lane. Although the compacted snow had smoothed out the potholes and my freezing trip was a short one, the wind, amplified by my speed, stabbed at my fingertips through inadequate knitted mittens, and my helmet exposed my ears to the onslaught until my head ached. I had underestimated the cold. Again.

Today's mission was to visit my favourite coffee spot. It felt a little insincere calling it my "favourite" as obviously, the coffee bar in the bookstore was my favourite. Had it not been, there would be something wrong with my business plan. But my *other* favourite cafe roasts coffee beans on site, and I needed to stock up, wholesale, to supply my own place. Gary, co-owner and "roast master" rarely speaks to anyone other than his seven-year-old daughter who is often hanging around in the cafe after school. It may be a language-barrier—the family are Chinese—but it occurs to me that I have never even seen him talk to his wife. He remains silent, enigmatic, and impossibly good at what he does. And today was "Roast Day."

The wind that battered my brain on route now transported a wonderful aroma of fresh roasting coffee throughout the City Square Plaza, noticeable even through my thick scarf. Even as a true coffee aficionado, I will admit that the smell of coffee is still better than its taste. The smell, to me, means comfort, inspiration and optimism, an intoxicating release from a miserable pandemic winter. I have learned time and time again that good things happen when I smell that scent. I am drawn to it, addicted. As I stumbled into the cafe half-blinded by the steam on my glasses, I am greeted by the joyful sight of a thousand little brown beans waltzing their way around the roasting drum, snapping and cracking in the heat, and getting shinier with every revolution. I buy a large bag of them and hug it to myself as I wait for Gary's talkative wife, Sunshine, to make my drink. The beans are still warm and turn the bag into a comforting pillow. The first sip of my velvety hot espresso and the quick chat with Sunshine makes the frigid trek more than worth it.

I like to believe that coffee and conversation bring people together. The original "penny universities" were the meeting places of wits and merchants and poets and pamphleteers and the occasional mad scientist, and they were places where inventive (and rowdy) conversations took on the form of casual entertainment. Even if the discourse was not always polite or friendly, it could happen in a social setting where there was some degree of public accountability, in an age where one's reputation was of paramount importance to one's social status.

This idea is in no way confined to 17th century London. There is a lovely "Saskatchewanism" that city dwellers often miss out on—the tradition of "coffee row." Many small prairie towns have one solitary diner—acting as coffee shop, restaurant, and sometimes as the lone bar as well. Coffee Row is the large table in these places where the locals gather to chat about life and the universe—all fuelled by "bottomless" cups of coffee. It may not sound much like the academic debates between London elites during the olden days, but it is where problems get solved; typical "rowers" may represent decades of farming experience gathered in one small establishment, and neighbours know that this is where to go if they ever need help. These places (and in more urban areas, the 24-hour Tim Hortons branches) are the Saskatchewan equivalent of the modern British pub: egalitarian, ubiquitous, community hubs. Even in the absence of cheap pints of warm beer, they are nonetheless intoxicating as you immerse yourself in the familiar surroundings. Coffee Row is also, of course, the local court of public opinion, which is an intimidating prospect in such small towns. Sometimes, I crave acceptance on the few coffee rows I've encountered, where I am still seen as an outsider. Other times, I miss the anonymity of over-crowded England.

In an increasingly mistrustful, anonymous, unkind, and disconnected world, any face-to-face discussion of ideas in a supportive and neutral environment has to be encouraged. This was what I wanted to create with my bookstore-cafe. I want to build a Coffee Row, but with books as conversation starters. And I want it to be the antithesis of Twitter.

Unfortunately, getting together for animated discussions with strangers over coffee was *exactly the wrong thing* to be doing in a pandemic. My trip to the roaster was brief, as it was closed to "sit-in" customers, and I had to gulp my espresso from a paper cup while huddled outside the cafe in the cold.

In the advent of the mask mandate, not long after we opened, we couldn't even chat "face to face." I saw that Astrid's eye make-up grew more elaborate as time progressed, but the bookstore had been open six months before I noticed that Ian actually has a beard. Whereas I had planned the store with a seating area for the coffee bar and had spent days with Rielle swearing while assembling the flat-packed chairs, it was rarely used.

It is often said that crises bring people together. Throughout 2020 in Canada, there were continual reminders in the media reminding everyone that "we are all in this together!"—yet for the most part, it was difficult to believe. The Covid-19 crisis did the exact opposite of bringing people together; it necessitated isolation, quarantine and keeping people apart. I do believe that this period of not being able to gather, socialise and be in the company of strangers is the real cause of a lot of the conspiracy theories, polarisation and online hate that we are enduring today. We are social creatures, and we need other people to maintain our humanity. Absence may make the heart grow fonder, but isolation makes the mind grow weirder.

Throughout all of this—the mandatory masks, social distancing, take-out-only coffee, contactless deliveries of online purchases, the construction of cohorts and "bubbles" of favoured companions to the exclusion of others—never once did I think that coffee shops would cease to exist. *Of course*, people would come back. After all, they had before.

In *The Diary of Samuel Pepys*, written in London during the bubonic plague in the 1660s, coffee houses were avoided by the risk-averse for fear of infection. In May 1665, Pepys wrote about a visit to a London coffeehouse: *where all the news is of the Dutch [fleet sailing] and of the plague growing upon us in this towne; and of remedies against it, some saying one thing, some another.* Confusion and misinformation about public health issues are not solely limited to the 2020s, it seems. Later, Pepys details the coffeehouses gradually closing during the worst months of the plague in London, and the general view being that *promiscuously conversing with one another, do readily propagate the infection.* King Charles II then issued a proclamation, saying, "No more alehouses be licensed than are *absolutely* necessary in each city." Being a fan of conversing promiscuously in those absolutely necessary pubs and coffeehouses myself, I can relate to and sympathise with Pepys on this one. His diary entry for February 1666 notes how, when he finally returned to his beloved coffeehouse with a friend after staying away for nearly a year, he was surprised to see the place *very full, and company it seems hath been there all the plague time.* There are always those who flout the rules, apparently.

In Saskatchewan, all cafes, coffee shops and restaurants were closed down for a few months in 2020, but our lockdown was short-lived—soon enough, they were allowed to re-open, albeit with capacity restrictions, social distancing, masks and later, proof of vaccination requirements. I was curious to see in Pepys' diary if coffeehouse patrons were worried about returning to them after the plague had abated. He notes that some were wary and were sure to ask whether anyone in an acquaintance's household were sick before sitting down with them for coffee. I was worried that even after the Premier of Saskatchewan lifted the restrictions, people would still stay away, either out of nervousness or merely having gotten used to everything being closed.

History suggests, however, that forcibly closing coffee shops seems to make people's desire to frequent them even stronger. During the days of the Ottoman Empire, several sultans tried to ban coffee shops, but none were successful for very long as they could not find many people willing to enforce the ban. King Charles II tried to close all the London coffeehouses in 1675, paranoid that the coffeehouse patrons were plotting against him. The fear was not unfounded, as coffeehouses were known to be full of dissenters and revolutionaries. However, the outcry from the ban became more of a threat to Charles's throne than the threat from seditious rumours that coffeehouse culture entertained, and so the ban was repealed, and King Charles resorted to taxing coffee heavily instead to dissuade people. That worked about as well as the "sin" tax on alcohol in present day Canada.

The day before Christmas Eve saw Astrid, Ian and I huddled in the coffee bar of our shop, in an illicit festive gathering. According to the provincial legislation, no public indoor gatherings were allowed, and we were only supposed to have gatherings of five people in our own homes. The three of us working together in the shop was perfectly lawful, but having a Christmas celebration together wasn't, because the virus obviously knew exactly when we turned the Closed sign around. Coronavirus can also tell the time apparently, because the bars had to stop selling off-sale alcohol at 10 p.m. After closing the store for the penultimate time before the holiday, I scurried across the road to the liquor store and grabbed some cans of a beer called "Book Club" from a local brewery as it seemed so apt. The three of us then ordered sushi from the restaurant next door. Very festive! Their dining room was closed, but if I walked the food ten feet between their door and ours, we could eat comfortably. We had to wear masks, but if we had food or a drink in our hands, we could take them off.

Secretly, behind the closed doors of our shuttered coffee shop, we enjoyed our meal naked-faced like the miscreants we were. I write this as a convoy of truckers, supposedly protesting the Federal government vaccine mandates, hold Ottawa under siege. These folks really do not like our Prime Minister, and it is easy to get drunk on righteous indignation when surrounded by like-minded, loud people. The convoy organisers are from Alberta but there is a strong Saskatchewan contingent too. That the protest was partially dreamed up and debated on a "coffee row" somewhere in a small town on the prairies is a fairly safe assumption. For better or worse, coffee places have always been and probably always will be, where revolutions begin.

I am lucky in that, unlike other small business owners, the majority of my stock does not have a sell-by date. I can afford to be patient. Samuel Pepys concluded that *delights, pleasant things, mirth, and diversions of course returned* to early modern London, as they will to our communities too. By

December 1665, Pepys noted that *to our great joy, the town fills apace, and shops begin to be open again.* The Great Plague of 1665 had little lasting effect on coffee shops and other intoxicating spaces, and I take comfort in the belief that the same will be true in the present day.

18
ANNABEL AND THE TERRIBLE, HORRIBLE, NO GOOD, VERY BAD DAY

Januarys in Saskatchewan wear us all down, eventually. New Year's celebrations were pandemic-muted and brief, the US election had not been the triumphant End of Trump that most had hoped for, and people's spirits were further mired by the January 6th insurrection. In Regina, the schools decided to have an extra week of "online learning" before returning to the classroom, so the kids were still hanging around at home, frustrated and bored. *Oh look, the virus is still here and it's snowing again.* The days were dark, and I was getting miserable.

Sylvia's final work on the bookstore building that should have included rebuilding our bathroom and kitchen area was to have been completed over the Christmas break. At the last minute, or so she said, one of the workers contracted Covid-19 and had to isolate over Christmas, so everything was postponed, once again. This week, it would be done, she promised. Doing so required turning the water supply off, so I arranged to open the shop just for the afternoons and to not serve coffee for the week while the water supply was interrupted. We would lose a bit of coffee income, but book sales would not be severely affected if we could stay partially open while the work was completed.

It did mean that Theia had to accompany me to work each afternoon. I maintain, online-kindergarten just isn't a plausible endeavour. I have spent most of the last few years trying to persuade Theia to come off her screens or not to watch too much TV, and now she was expected to tune into (well-intentioned) videos from her Kindergarten teacher every weekday. I made the decision early on in the school year that I would not enforce this. If Theia was interested, then we would watch together, but if she didn't want to, I was not going to try to persuade her.

On this particular Terrible, Horrible, No Good, Very Bad Day, Theia wanted to come with me to the dollar store as I had to pick up a few supplies for the shop before I opened for the day. Theia is very fond of the dollar store, partially because it was the one place that stayed open during the lockdown that we could go to as an *outing*, but mainly because I tended to overcompensate for the miserable world by buying her cheap plastic crap each time we visited. This time, she found a Unicorn pen, made extra special because the rubber unicorn head on the end of the pen flashed and lit up when you squeezed it. I agreed to get it for her thinking it would keep her amused and scribbling while I worked in the bookstore that afternoon. The trouble started, however, when Theia couldn't decide between the pink pen or the purple pen. Such a difficult decision! I gave her five minutes to make her mind up while I did the rest of the shopping, and told her firmly that if she couldn't decide, she should put both of them back and choose something else. She whined about that and was still clutching both pens by the time we got to the cash desk.

I rang one unicorn pen through the self-checkout machine and told Theia to put the other one back *right now*. Theia stood stock-still in the middle of the aisle and *howled* like the world was ending.

I took the pink pen from her and handed her the purple one which I had paid for—all the while becoming more cross at her public outburst. Then I returned the pink pen to the shelf. She started wailing so loudly one of the shop assistants came over and kindly asked Theia if she would like a pink one instead. I told her firmly that she was not getting both. Theia screamed—pure rage-filled noise, no longer capable of coherent speech— and all over a stupid pen. Except, of course, it wasn't about the pen. It was about tiredness and cold and lack of routine and anxiety about everything and wearing a mask to go shopping and school only being on a screen and not seeing her friends and no dance class and no parks and Christmas being over too soon. And I was irritated about the pen and the yelling but was also feeling exhausted and hopeless and worried and frustrated and socially awkward and angry at myself for not being in control of all those things. I dragged her out of there still screeching as if she were being tortured, all the while feeling like the worst mother in the world.

She kept it up too, the child has immense lung capacity. She cried hysterically, breathlessly, uncontrollably, all the way down Scarth Street. I was taken aback by the sheer drama. If I had not already forced her out of the shop, I probably would have given in and bought both of the damn things—was a couple of dollars' worth all this trauma? But I had reached my limit and all I could do was to remove her from the situation and hope that was enough to calm her down. I fought her into the bike seat still sobbing, and she bawled all the way to the bookstore.

When we got there, I chained the bike up outside the shop, lifted Theia out and crouched to her level, asking her to take deep breaths until she could stop crying. I said I would call her father to come pick her up if she couldn't calm down because I couldn't handle much more. That at least did the trick. Evidently, Daddy posed more of a threat than I do. Theia snivelled and said quietly that she still wanted to stay with me. We hugged.

And then, fumbling for my store keys, I thought to check my phone.

A terse text from Sylvia: *The front door to the shop was left open!*

I was incredulous. I trusted Astrid implicitly and was sure she was not careless enough to leave it open. She had locked up every night for five months without issue. I stumbled into the shop through the back door with a dejected Theia trailing behind me.

The security alarm had been triggered at the building that morning which meant that someone had tried to break in and that the door must have been unlocked since Astrid left at 6 p.m. the previous evening. If the door had been left unlocked, let alone left open, Astrid should not have been able to set the alarm—yet it had to have been set, or how else could it have been triggered?

Sylvia barged into the shop as soon as she heard us arrive and started yelling at me. Leaving the door not fully closed was utterly unacceptable to her, and she demanded that Astrid give her key back. She also threatened to charge me for the costs of getting the alarm codes reset so that Astrid could not disable the alarm without supervision.

Of course, the return of Astrid's key would mean me having to come and unlock the building every morning and lock up every evening, six days a week, with the kids in tow, with no car, in the snow. I could not run a business like that—and told Sylvia so.

This started an all-out argument. Somehow, Sylvia's narrative flicked from the alarm system to the floors, which she claimed were too dirty and that I was damaging them—*her property!*—by not cleaning them. She even told me that customers wouldn't come in because of it. This almost rendered me speechless—not only was it entirely untrue, as Astrid and I mopped them every night as people trudged melted snow through the door all winter—but it was also blatantly none of her business. The whole point of all that waxing that had delayed my opening by three months was that the wax protects the floor underneath it. The floor may not have been as shiny as when it was brand new, but that was because it was being trodden upon by *my* customers in *my* shop. Did Sylvia really expect them to levitate across the room?

I blinked a bit in stunned silence, but then managed to turn the tables and asked Sylvia why, as she was so concerned about the upkeep of her property, did we still not have a bathroom or kitchen after five months? I could see no evidence that the work had even been started. Sylvia claimed she didn't have sufficient funds to order the work done. I asked what had happened to the four-figure rent I paid her the week before.

Mercifully, a customer came in at that point and so I quite literally pushed Sylvia out the back door. I managed to control myself enough to help the man find a copy of *1984* and upsold *Brave New World* with it. (I can't imagine why those two are so popular at the moment!) I was reeling from Sylvia's onslaught, my heart racing as I rang his card through the debit machine. As soon as we were alone again, I sat with Theia on the couch and cuddled her until we both felt better about the world. I was close to tears, but Theia, entirely oblivious, was drawing snowflakes with her new unicorn pen.

I sat, processing the situation until Astrid came in to relieve me. I felt like I couldn't go on paying full rent on a building that no longer had the facilities that had been there when I signed the lease. That constant feeling of walking on eggshells around Sylvia, anxious of her next explosive outburst, did nothing for morale either. But then, what choice did I have? I did not know what to do.

With as much tranquility as I could muster, I asked Astrid about the unlocked door. She looked aghast and insisted that she'd locked it. Confused—and immediately suspicious of Sylvia—I asked Astrid to show me how she locked up. I still did not understand how she had managed to set the alarm with the door open, as it was programmed not to arm itself until the door was in the locked position. Making sure the alarm was definitely disabled this time, Astrid demonstrated how she locked and unlocked the front door, which is how I realised what had happened. Astrid was locking the door, but not using the deadbolt (which required a separate manoeuvre of jigging the mechanism, not immediately intuitive when locking from the inside.) So, the door had been locked all along, just not deadbolted. The alarm had been triggered presumably when a customer had come by and pushed the door hard, expecting us to be open at our usual earlier time. Despite all Sylvia's outrage, the building had been secure the entire time.

Discovering this fact did little to improve my mood; if anything it worsened my already terrible opinion of Sylvia. I did, however, remember which literary character Sylvia most reminded me of. It's Mrs Wisbeach from George Orwell's *Keep the Aspidistra Flying*. Orwell's nightmare landlady floats around the halls of her dismal tenement building, grumbling at her tenants' comings and goings, and so suspicious of every creak that the main character resorts to wrapping the crockery in newspaper to make a cup of tea, so that the chinks do not awaken her wrath. Yes, this suddenly felt very familiar. I can only hope that Astrid never becomes Gordon Comstock, frustrated artist and Mrs Wisbeach's tenant who eeks out a depressing existence working for pennies in a run-down bookstore. We are indeed living in an Orwellian age. Just not the dystopian portrayed in Orwell's *1984*.

As I cycled home with a now fully-recovered Theia, I passed the old lingerie shop building on 13th Avenue, opposite the Cathedral. I was cycling directly into the sunset, which coupled with the snow glare, was blinding. So maybe it was just coincidence that I was looking to the side of the road not straight ahead, or maybe it was fate, but that afternoon I noticed a massive FOR LEASE sign on the lingerie shop window.

In Judith Viorst's *Alexander and the Terrible, Horrible, No Good, Very*

Bad Day, there is no happy ending. Alexander does not go to bed with all his frustrations from the day resolved. His mum just says, "Some days are like that." It's true. Some days are awful.

But other days are not.

19
STILL AIR THAT BITES

At a certain point in the year, every year, I find myself trying to open doors with my elbow. This is because seemingly every single time I touch inanimate objects in winter, I get a static shock. So frequent are the shocks that my reactions become utterly irrational and paranoid. I do know that I am just as likely to get a shock on my elbow as I am on my fingers, but somehow I convince myself that my sleeve will soften the sensation. It doesn't, and I just look crazy. The static is most likely a result of cheap polyester rugs (at home and in the bookstore) building up a charge against nonslip rubber soled shoes, but it is much more of an issue in winter because the air is so dry. It is also dry enough for me to be constantly thirsty, and to buy copious amounts of lip balm, hand cream and conditioner to alleviate my papery skin and straw-like hair. Saskatchewan is fairly parched anyway being such a long way from the more temperate coasts, but in winter every drop of moisture is frozen from the air until the world sparkles and crackles with cold.

For the past nine winters, I have tried to accurately describe the cold in Saskatchewan to my UK friends and family. With no prior experience of anything below -5°C, my British friends can't quite grasp what -30°C feels like. Eventually I tendered the task out to my Canadian writer friends, and one suggested: Still air that bites. I like this; in the minus twenties, the outside air is cold enough to freeze your skin even before you factor in the windchill. It's not like you can "get out of the wind" to warm up, the cold creeps in everywhere, and it is dangerous. The response to this from Britain was less elegant: "Are you bonkers? Why the hell did you move somewhere where it's -30? That's colder than my freezer!"

Unlike in the UK, where half an inch of snow brings the country to a standstill, life just continues in the bleak prairie winter. The kids rarely get "snow days" off school. Public transport, such as it is in Regina, pushes its way slowly through the drifts, skating rinks are built, and people just wear more clothes and get on with it. That is not to say they don't moan about it, and there is also that first week of winter every year where everyone seemingly forgets how to drive—but for the most part the cold is seen as a mere inconvenience, and inevitable.

Even after nearly a decade here, I still feel 'new' enough to get excited by the cold. It is a unique experience, and always an adventure. I do my best to embrace it. My bike is kitted out for winter riding, I have gradually taught myself if not to skate well, then at least not to break my ankle at the rink. I make a point of taking the children down to the Only Hill in Regina to go tobogganing with their friends. I have a woolly hat (toque) in every colour. Yet whenever I express this seasonal excitement, I am met with derision from local friends. "You are such an immigrant, Annabel!" Saskatchewanians do not appreciate their amazing winters.

Although Canada is somewhat famous for its cold and the sport of hockey, in literature the snow is often depicted as a dangerous dark force. I read Peter Hoeg's *Miss Smilla's Feeling for Snow* as a teen, which is one of the earliest popular Nordic noir novels set in the Greenland arctic and amongst the Greenlandic Inuit. While not actually Canadian, this is the first book I read where snow was anything other than "pretty" and fun to play in. In Canada, Cold noir seems to be a genre unto itself. I can see why.

Moon of the Crusted Snow, a Canadian bestseller by Waubgeshig Rice is a chilling account of isolation in an already vulnerable community on a First Nation in Northern Ontario, following an unknown apocalypse. The fact that the source of the apocalypse is never explained makes it all the more unnerving, and you start to look at your neighbours suspiciously after reading it. *Polar Vortex* by Shani Mootoo is another one: the snow smothers things and secrets are hidden in it. The cold is a terrifying villain, beautiful but deadly, and it can hold you captive.

At 6:30 a.m., CBC Radio Saskatchewan woke me with the "news" (at this point in the season, it's not new) that there is yet another Extreme Cold Warning and the temperature outside is in the -30s with windchills in the -40s. Joy! Just what I needed. That day, I had to navigate out to the east end of Regina on the bus to get supplies for the coffee side of bookstore operations. The radio piece then continued with an "In Your Shoes" segment where they sent an intrepid journalist to navigate Regina's public transit in the snow.

Predictably, he's late for work, misses bus connections and discovers that taking the bus takes more than twice the time that driving does. Then, halfway through the day, he gives up because he doesn't want his kid freezing to death waiting half an hour for a bus in the extreme cold. I am certainly not going to condemn him for that—no one should be out for that length of time when it is so dangerously cold, particularly not a child when you have other options. But, and this is a big BUT: he had other options. He got his wife to come pick them up. In a car.

Having successfully forced both my own children into snowsuits and masks and out the door and to school on time, I begin to run my errands. Just as I leave the school, I see my bus pass the end of our block. It stops opposite me, and I frantically jaywalk to get to it before it pulls away from the bus stop. I don't quite make it. As it pulls out, I run and manage to knock on the back window. Fortunately, it stops, and I jump on. "Try not to bang on the bus, eh?" says the driver. I apologise, and she shrugs from behind the clear plexiglass Covid-19 protection screen. Hardly the first time anyone has done that, I imagine. I glance at my phone. 8:47 a.m. According the city of Regina bus transit schedule, the bus should have passed at 8:51 a.m.

The driver is the same woman who runs that route most mornings. She is one of the mighty few who are genuinely chipper and cheery in the early morning, even in winter. From behind her mask and toque, she tells everyone, "Have a good day!" and "Make good choices!" as they leave the bus, along with "See you tomorrow!" She knows all the regular commuters. She knows some of us by name, particularly the kids. As we near the downtown bus shelters, she yells, "We're about five minutes early, so plenty of time for coffee!"

Sadly, five minutes early translates into a fifteen-minute wait for me, as my connection is still running to schedule. Fortunately, the downtown bus stops are heated. Slightly. There is a tall lanky teenager at the bus shelter with me. Thin runners instead of boots, no gloves and only a hoodie on over a t-shirt. He is shaking with cold. Unlike Milo's refusal to wear hideously uncool snowpants, I don't think the outfit is a fashion choice. It might be all he has. He's only there for a few more minutes though, until his bus arrives. My bus pulls in next, and I am transported right to the door of where I wanted to be.

Shopping done, the return journey is equally arduous and no less cold.

And this time I am carrying enormous bags of coffee cups and industrial quantities of hot chocolate powder. The #12 bus goes along the major road on the north edge of the Cathedral neighbourhood, which is the closest I can get without having to wait for forty minutes for the 13th Avenue bus. I press the bell as we get into Cathedral and the bus halts next to a random pole on the edge of the busy road. The door opens and I am faced with a snowbank that reaches to my thighs. I make a jump for it, and my deep boot prints show that I am the first person to have used this "bus stop" in days.

Even if there was a sidewalk here, I'd struggle to climb over to it. I have decent boots, I'm tall and fairly fit and healthy. Also, I didn't have the kids with me on this excursion. Still, getting off the road and trudging up to the end of the block through that depth of snow took a lot of effort. Got a kid in a stroller? Mobility difficulties? No money for snow boots? You're screwed, basically.

The cold makes even the shortest journey seem like a voyage through the Northwest Passage. It is exhausting; the extra energy needed to just keep my body at a normal healthy temperature when walking outside makes me incredibly hungry, grouchy and run down. This is how it traps you: even if the buses are running, the cold can keep you captive just by sapping all your mental and physical energy long before you succumb to actual hypothermia. Just putting on all the extra layers needed to get out of the door safely requires enormous effort and forward planning. There are no quick, spur of the moment outings in a Saskatchewan winter.

Or are there? For my birthday in February 2021, we decided to do just that. Fed up with Sylvia's antics, the worrying lack of customers willing to risk frostbite to come book shopping, online schooling, and the ice ruts on the streets of Regina, we decided to take a break. Unable to go anywhere too exotic because of Covid-19, we settled on Cypress Hills Provincial Park in the southwest of Saskatchewan. There were trees, a few things that could be called hills from a distance, heated, "winterised" cabins in the woods and, we hoped, plenty of wholesome winter activities to enjoy.

But we did not expect that level of cold.

Little did we know that we had set off into what was going to be the coldest weekend of the year, with record-breaking temperatures and windchills in the minus mid-50s. Not for the first time, it was "warmer" on the surface of Mars. I took a screenshot of the temperature on my phone to send to our niece in South Africa, who was experiencing similar temperatures without the minus sign at her home on the edge of the Kalahari Desert. Previously, I had mailed her a copy of Robert Munsch's *50 Below Zero* for her kids—I don't think she ever realised the premise of the book is based on bitter experience.

We skated, and discovered a new phenomenon that tested the laws of physics as we know them. Ice skating is possible because the pressure of your weight on the thin steel blade lowers the melting point of the top layer of ice, causing it to melt. The skate can then glide on a thin layer of water that instantly refreezes as soon as you've passed by. However, if you attempt this when the ambient temperature is much below -30°C, the pressure from the blade is not strong enough to melt the ice. We were reduced to half-walking, half-skidding around the rink, the skates making a painful squeaking noise as we moved in the cold, surreal world.

The Resort at Cypress Hills was stunningly beautiful; the soft blanket of snow between trees outlined with hoar frost made everything magical and glittering. We saw more deer than people. No CBC news filled with doom and gloom, no shovelling to be done, and no phone signal to keep me constantly on edge about book orders arriving late. It was everything I needed and more. Our admiration of the place was restricted to short bursts though, followed by long periods of sheltering and recuperating indoors. We went sledding on real hills (as opposed to a small slope by the creek in Regina). Milo even found a luge track that someone had kindly constructed in the snow and spent a happy afternoon careening round it. Theia cried from the cold as her snowboots did not withstand the extremes of temperature as well as our adult versions, but five minutes in the car with hot chocolate and the heating on full blast was enough to warm and cheer her up again.

Despite the temperature, I decided I must make the most of this brief time away, and, leaving Carl and the kids huddled up in blankets playing Uno, I tried out my birthday present from Carl—snowshoes! I merrily stomped around one of the shorter marked trails at the resort, the snowshoes helping me scale a few hills and preventing me sliding down the other side. I even saw several snowshoe hares, hopping along much faster than I was. My scarf wound around my face forced my breath up onto my glasses, which consequently fogged up and then froze, so I took them off. I didn't need to read much out in the leafless forest. With no lenses to protect my eyes, I soon got a stylish makeover with Canadian Mascara: my eyelashes froze into white spikes that matched my hair that had already frozen grey. I can now see why so many fairy tales have a wicked witch with long grey hair living in the woods; just a series of poor women, cold and grouchy about the weather, that turned to the dark side.

When we reluctantly tried to leave, we discovered that the cold had other ideas. There were only a few electric plug-ins for block heaters in the parking lot at the resort and we hadn't managed to plug the car in overnight. Mercifully, it started on the third try, but it was not happy. The parking lot was at the bottom of a steep slope covered with compacted snow. Even when we got the car moving, Carl found he could not coax it up the slope. Like most Canadian vehicles, it is an automatic, and it was stuck in first gear. Carl is not a mechanic, but he is an excellent problem solver, and soon diagnosed the problem. The transmission fluid had become viscous with the cold and so the transmission couldn't change gears quick enough to scale the hill. This, he realised, could be resolved by driving the car round and round in circles in the parking lot until the engine warmed sufficiently to thin out the transmission fluid. We received several bemused looks from the nearby cross-country skiers, who wondered why we appeared to be joyriding in a minivan at 10 a.m. at a top speed of 15 km per hour.

Winter is a powerful and unknowable beast; brutal, merciless and inescapable, and yet beautiful, strangely serene and always an adventure. Knowing the inevitability of its coming, and recognising the dangers it poses to people, vehicles and sanity, I will always choose to embrace winter. The cold is a risky thrill to chase; beware the air that bites.

20
THE PLASTIC BOX
THAT BROKE US

When I was growing up in the early 1990s, my parents enforced Sunday mornings as their time to relax and listen to their music. They would put on a selection from Dad's enormous collection of records, CDs and cassettes, and read the paper while gently bouncing in their fidgety bentwood armchairs from Ikea. It sounds like a cosy, idyllic time, but the chosen soundtrack to these mornings was anything but peaceful.

My dad has an odd taste in music. Most of it could loosely fit into the prog-rock genre but accompanied by a good helping of Eastern European folk music and the occasional theremin. My husband refers to it all as "Circus Music." (I imagine I am a source of constant disappointment to my dad, as I have never embraced any of his music. In fact, I have barely kept up an interest in *any* music into adulthood, beyond a vague preference for angsty indie bands with political lyrics.)

I wanted to have background music in the bookstore—without it, I worried it would turn into a library with everyone speaking in hushed tones. It was fascinating to see how, when the store was quiet and there were few people in, they seemed to automatically lower their voices whenever they spoke. Perhaps there is something about being in the presence of so many books that inspires an awed silence. That silence can quickly become awkward though, so I wanted to fill it, but I knew it could be tricky to do this effectively. I have worked in coffee shops long enough to have come to loathe the nondescript soft jazz that permeates those places, and equally, the well-intentioned inoffensive indie playlists that cool, hipster cafes play. I am also acutely aware of how annoying tunes can be when you must listen to the same thing for eight hours a day, every day. In that environment, even your favourite songs get stuck in your head until all the joy is sapped from them. So, no soft jazz, no hipster indie, and no earworms, and nothing that distracted the customer too much from the books. It also had to be cheerful, upbeat and tolerable to everyone. I now understand why hotel lobbies play panpipe classics: no one likes it, but no one really hates it either.

I decided to ask my dad for suggestions, and together we settled on a few albums by the Penguin Cafe Orchestra (who, despite the name, are described as *Avant-pop*), Sigur Ros (largely instrumental, Icelandic and strange) and a band called Japonize Elephants (who claim on their website to make "Hardcore-gypsy-circus-klezmer-pirate-clown-madness for everyone!") I have definitely made people *notice* the music, if nothing else. Unfortunately, given I was playing these on repeat during one of the hardest times in the bookstore's short history, I now can't help associating the melodies with freezing, frustration, and anxiety.

Sigur Ros, with their eerie and surreal soundscapes of Iceland, definitely captured the zeitgeist of the early part of 2021. Temperatures in the -30s do happen every year, but not, if memory serves, for quite so long a period. Not only are January and February hard times in retail generally, the pandemic certainly did not help the situation, and then the weather seemed determined to finish us off entirely. In the dark and frigid "dead" of winter, it is easier to believe in malevolent, supernatural forces conspiring against you.

Speaking of which, the situation with our landlady did not improve.

One of the many, many little things that were never finished in the bookstore building was the mailbox. In fact, Sylvia seemed intent on leaving figurative and literal holes in every project she undertook. There was a large hole in the wall where a panel was supposed to have been fitted to cover the electrical breakers. I had resorted to hiding it behind a poster. Some of the vent covers were also missing, leaving holes large enough to be dangerous. After spending so long fussing about the floor tiles, Sylvia only replaced the longer vent covers when I physically fell in one and gashed my ankle badly enough to bleed all over the fresh floor wax. (I still have the scar.) She eventually made sure these were covered the day before we opened, but the smaller floor vents by the walls were left uncovered, requiring me to place chairs over them to prevent others from acquiring the same injury.

It was the mailbox that caused the most significant issue, however. Mainly because there wasn't one. Instead, there was a substantial hole in the door panel, open to the street, where a mail slot should have been fitted with a box behind it to collect the mail. A missing mailbox may not sound the most insurmountable of problems, but when you are experiencing windchills nearing -50°C, any hole that let the wind in was a serious concern. To make matters worse, we were entirely reliant on Sylvia to call in the experts to fix it; the door was glass, and not something I felt comfortable drilling into by myself.

We did ask her, remind her, and practically beg her to fix it. It was already desperately quiet in the store, and the last thing I needed was customers being put off by the unpleasant temperatures in the shop as well as outside it. It was not an easy thing to hide, as when I opened up in the mornings, I had to scrape ice off the *inside* of the windows. Sylvia attempted to reassure me that she'd get her favoured handyman to come do it "soon." In the meantime, she offered me an alternative solution: a giant purple blanket.

"Your favourite colour!" she smiled, unconvincingly. The woollen blanket was indeed a lovely shade of lilac and, according to its $3.99 Value Village price tag, was a steal of a deal. But I wasn't sure what I was supposed to be doing with it. Sylvia, seemingly put out by my lack of appreciation for her generosity and lack of understanding of her innate ingenuity, briskly demonstrated that the blanket was to be used to block the hole. She folded the blanket and shoved half of it into the missing mail slot, leaving the rest to trail on the floor in the shop's entrance. She then disappeared back up to her warm and toasty office on the second floor. No handyman ever appeared to rectify the situation.

The blanket, although marginally better than having a large gap open to the elements, did little to improve the temperature inside the shop. My mornings were cold and miserable with few customers, and so uncomfortable even the "circus music" couldn't lift my spirits. Sometimes, I could see my breath when I sat at the computer desk. I tried to keep warm by drinking copious amounts of hot coffee, but then that made me need to go to the toilet—which was still missing seven months after it was supposed to have been replaced. Bathroom breaks required leaving the shop unattended and marching up the stairs to "Sylvia's floor" to use the bathroom in the office above the main shop. Every morning would be a difficult choice between the urgent need to pee, and the urge to avoid Sylvia for as long as possible. This only increased my stress levels and added to the deteriorating landlady-tenant relationship.

Astrid does not like the cold, and she found herself even less able to tolerate the temperature in the shop than I could. Astrid's method of managing the temperature issues was to just to crank up the heating. Our utilities were included with the rent, so an increased heating bill would only affect Sylvia, and hopefully, spur her into action. The vent that I had so dramatically fallen in was right by our counter and, for a few days, Astrid and I enjoyed standing right on top of the warm draught. I did not understand the thermostat settings as they were in Fahrenheit, but as the store was so big and the outside air so cold, we had to set it to 80°F to get it anywhere near tolerable in the shop.

Needless to say, Sylvia was not impressed by this. As soon as she returned to the building after a weekend, she told Astrid off for "messing" with the heating, complaining it was too hot in her office. She turned the heating down again and stomped off. Astrid waited thirty minutes, then turned it back up again. This time, Sylvia told her she was being silly and to just put a sweater on. Astrid wisely said nothing and shivered her way through the afternoon. Then, when she was sure Sylvia had left the building for the day, she turned it up again. Although I was well aware of the problem, I received a series of text messages from Astrid who wished to document the situation. She took pictures of the ice on the windows, and the temperature display on her phone. With the heating on at a level set by Sylvia, the inside temperature in our store was just 12°C at midday. I advised her to just keep turning the thermostat up whenever she could. This ridiculous game of cat and mouse continued for another day, until … Sylvia snapped.

On Day 3 of the Thermostat Wars, Astrid was on the opening shift, and I got a flurry of texts:

Annabel!

Annabel!

Annabel!

OMG.

You have got to see this!

A picture message slowly downloaded.

Astrid had arrived in the freezing building, to find a clear plastic box screwed to the wall, fully covering the thermostat. On the side of the box was a lock that would allow anyone with a key to get at the controls, but it was certainly tough enough to keep us out. I had to laugh! Sylvia had obviously levelled up her game, and I couldn't help but admire the sheer magnitude of her pettiness. Surely, the effort required to source the plastic box, mount it on the wall, and have a lock fixed on it would have been greater than just fitting the mailbox and solving the heating problem altogether. It took a special sort of passive aggression to go to all that trouble, and I chose to feel honoured that she'd gone to those lengths just to annoy me.

I briefly considered finding a screwdriver to remove the box, but then I remembered I was an adult. Enough was enough, we couldn't continue like this. I had lost any hope of Sylvia doing the renovations by this point, and all her passive-aggressive behaviour and potential mafia family connections meant that there was no repairing the situation with her. I knew she and I would never develop any respect for each other, but that was not the issue— her behaviour was starting to affect the business. We had no choice—the situation was untenable and if I wanted to save my business, it was time to leave. So, I called a lawyer. And then I called the realtor who was still listing the lingerie shop on 13th Avenue. She was very happy to hear from *me*.

One of my dad's less-circussy, but no less strange, CDs was a 1991 rock opera version of Edgar Allen Poe's gothic horror, *The Fall of the House of Usher*, performed by Peter Hammill. The short story, first published in *Burton's Gentleman's Magazine* in 1839 was rife with themes of insanity. As a teenager, I had never liked this CD as, to my uneducated ears, it was 75 minutes of sombre, melodramatic warbling, and I did not take the time to listen to the words. However, some twenty-five years later, I looked it up again thinking an operatic version of classic literature may fit in with the bookstore vibe. To date, I have never subjected either my staff or my customers to it in its entirety, but I have, at long last, actually listened to it attentively. It is creepier than I ever gave it credit for.

Somehow, our team survived until March in the frigid building and with my relationship with Sylvia growing ever more icy. By now, she had blocked my phone number and had not responded to any email communication from me for over a month. (Though she did pick up the rent payment without fail.)

Over the last cold month of winter, I had focused on a solution to my dire landlady situation. I had worked out an escape plan and it was beautiful in its simplicity. The plan was to do nothing—and wait for the lease to expire. I discovered, gleefully, that Sylvia's negligence had at last caught up with her. I had signed a one-year lease in March 2020, pre-pandemic. As I had not managed to open in that spring because of lockdowns (and Sylvia's lengthy delays with the flooring), we had written an addendum to the lease, extending it from September 2020 to August 2021. But, whether out of spite or apathy, *Sylvia had never signed the addendum.* I checked with my lawyer for safety's sake, and he confirmed that I was correct—without her signature on the addendum, the original lease took precedence, and that lease was just about to expire.

Sylvia was not reading my emails, but she did suddenly take notice of a letter from my lawyer. She was absolutely livid. If things had been bad before, they were now indescribably worse. Astrid and I were almost afraid to be in the building alone, knowing The Godmother was glowering down at us from above. Now, my dad's CD, *The Fall of the House of Usher*, did seem unnervingly relevant. Amid a terrifying rush of lawyers and stress and arguments with Sylvia, I was overcome with crippling self-doubt and fear, haunted by my very surroundings. We had to close the shop at a time when I needed to save every penny I could get; I struggled to pay a removal company and scrape together the deposit on the new building. I could feel my business, and myself, almost withering away inside the confines of the accursed place.

At last, moving day arrived four days before my lease expired, and we loaded as much as we could into a truck for its epic voyage to safety, four blocks down the road. We worked solidly for six hours straight, back and forth and back and forth, Astrid and the moving company workers loading at one end, Ian and I unloading at the other. The moving company, although more efficient than I could ever have hoped for, could not transport loose books, and we simply had not had the time to pack everything neatly in boxes. At 2:30 p.m., just as the removal company shut the doors on the truck for the last time, Sylvia appeared … and all hell broke loose.

For someone who seemed so determined to make our lives miserable in that building, she really didn't want us to leave either. Shouting and threatening us with all sorts of legal action, she finally demanded that we get out of her premises by 5 p.m. that night, and anything left in the space after that would become her property. I looked around at the mess of paperbacks tipped all over the floor, knowing that some of them would have to make the ultimate sacrifice. I called Marin with her truck—the same wonderful friend who'd helped me move everything into the building just a few months before—and we loaded as much as we could. I threw many more books into my cargo bike and trailed after the truck, pedalling frantically, but in the end, we knew we had to cut our losses. Working out what Sylvia would do with more than thirty copies of the same Young Adult books was beyond me, and I took a little solace in the thought that she'd have as much clearing up to do the next day as I would in my new place.

The utter chaos of moving the entire store in one day, and only six months after we'd first opened, was enough to drive me to madness. It felt as if the bookstore building itself came alive just to terrorise us with the cold and to reap revenge for so many maintenance jobs left unfinished. Sylvia, like the insane Madeline Usher, had haunted the place malevolently, ramping up the tension until we could suffer the fears no longer. Then, in one macabre, cataclysmic implosion on our moving day, the whole store was swallowed into an eternal abyss.

Our House of Usher had fallen.

21
COLOURFUL HIPSTER-DOOFUSES

In the early 2000s, we lived in a grey, wet and miserable little town in northeast England called Darlington. After years of hearing people scream at each other across the fences, and seeing flashing police lights every night, we began to actively avoid our neighbours, with whom I felt we had little in common.

With my love of colour and dubious fashion sense, our pet ferrets (who'd escaped into the neighbourhood more than once), and my beloved old motorbike (named "Binky" after Death's horse in the Discworld Series) out in front of our house, we were definitely marked as "the weird couple" on our street and usually left alone. At first, we hardly noticed—none of my friends knew their neighbours either—but it soon grew lonely and isolating, especially when Milo was born. There was little help for me when I struggled to adapt to being a new mum and few other families with small children with whom I could make friends.

The ways in which the local environment sometimes encroached on our little bubble were unfortunately, unwelcome.

At 2:00 a.m. one night, our neighbour started banging on our door frantically, yelling, "Aaron's trying to take your bike!" she said.

Sure enough, my motorbike was gone from the curb.

Aaron was a local teenaged delinquent who enjoyed petty theft and vandalism. Carl and I trooped outside in pyjamas, assuming Aaron wouldn't have gotten far yet. We were then joined by another neighbour from further up the street. Everyone loves a good late-night drama, but her appearance was made even more alarming by the fact that she was covered in blood.

"Yeah, Aaron was 'round earlier," she said. "He wanted to borrow a crowbar, you know, to get the chain off. I couldn't find one."

She obviously hadn't thought this was a reason to raise a red flag, and I was concerned about what could have happened if she had managed to find a crowbar for him. Then Carl dared to ask her about the blood.

"Oh, don't worry," she said. "It's not mine. My boyfriend was being an arse so I headbutted him."

Binky the bike was eventually recovered in a ditch by the railway bridge. Having not been able to remove the lock without a crowbar, Aaron had only been able to push the bike so far before the chain became wrapped around the wheel and stopped him from moving forward. I notified the police and the incident was added to Aaron's existing file of misdemeanours. (One of his first offences was scrawling his name in green spray paint on the railway bridge. When he was arrested, he asked the police how they knew it was him.)

This drama, along with many similar experiences, was what eventually drove us to move overseas. We loosely aimed for Canada, but the push to leave Darlington was far stronger than the pull to any specific location in Canada, especially Regina, a city we knew nothing about at the time.

Ten years later, I found that one of the bestselling fiction novels in The Penny University Bookstore is Less, by Andrew Sean Greer. In the book, failed novelist Arthur Less embarks on a trip halfway round the world, not because he has a real desire to travel, but purely to avoid going to his ex's wedding. When I think back on my own emigration adventures, (or, when I am asked to explain it to other people), I can relate to Arthur Less rather more easily than I'd like. I too went to ridiculous lengths just to escape Darlington, and there is something rather liberating about the certainty that you will never run into any exes, or people with whom you went to high school, that emigration brings. Having survived the lengthy and expensive process of emigration, my small family comfortably settled in the Cathedral neighbourhood and my experience here has been overwhelmingly positive. We have very little reason to avoid people here.

Here, an unexpected knock on the door doesn't lead to instant trepidation. One evening, a neighbour from the other side of the block knocked on our door, amiably introduced himself and thrust a flyer printed on bright yellow paper into my hand. "We thought we should have a block party for Canada Day. You've got kids, haven't you? Bring them along!"

That was the first of many annual block parties. The Covid-19 pandemic put paid to our Canada Day celebrations in 2020, but our neighbours were keen to adapt. Instead of inviting the whole block out onto the road, we opted for a socially distanced "Back Alley BBQ night." Each family dragged a barbecue into our shared alley, and cooked their food separately that year. The night was spent sitting in lawn chairs having very loud conversations with our neighbours to bridge the gap, literally and figuratively, between our houses.

The local kids, home from school, isolating and bored out of their minds, jumped at the opportunity to hang out with someone other than Mum and Dad. Soon there were bike races weaving in and out of the barbecues; the obligatory six-foot distancing suddenly coming in very handy to avoid being run over. It was a lovely, if brief, respite from the lonely lockdown.

The pandemic reaffirmed what I already knew: emigrating has been the best decision we ever made. I was confident that no one at that barbecue would ever ask to borrow a crowbar at 2:00 a.m. We may not have grown up in this city, or even on this continent, but we seem to have far more in common with the people next door in Regina than we ever did in our "hometown" of Darlington.

My little bit of Regina—and I do admit that without a car, my world is pretty small—is one of the most colourful bits and has a reputation for containing the arty, hipster and weird neighbourhoods, all rather at odds with the dominant prairie culture. Certainly, in comparison with Darlington, it is also affluent and acutely middle class. "Cathedral" (so called because there is a big cathedral in the middle of it) is one of the few places in Regina where you can exist without a car fairly easily, because everything you need is within walking distance, and the downtown core is easily accessible for work. There is a plethora of cyclists in this neighbourhood, and I have even seen a tandem parked outside one of the coffee shops, and a bearded man with a man bun on a giant unicycle careening down the road. Cathedral does deserve its reputation as the "land of hipster-doofuses"—as the rest of the city apparently views us.

Tree-lined streets keep the residential blocks beautiful all year round. It is one of the oldest neighbourhoods in Regina, and that is made obvious by its architecture. In 1912, most of the city was levelled by a tornado (a highly unusual event, as Saskatchewan is situated well above "tornado alley" that bisects the US to the south of us). The Cathedral survived, but most of the houses were destroyed and rebuilt the following year. This makes most of this neighbourhood (our house included) just over a century old, but with newer builds—like the bookshop—squeezed in between. An element of Canadian cities that I imagine many British people can appreciate is the very relaxed planning regulations. Especially in this area, there is no obligation to build new developments in the same style as the existing buildings, no cookie-cutter designs where every house has to look like the one next to it. It is wonderfully affirming to me to realise that, if left to their own devices, people will paint their houses purple or primrose-yellow, they will construct a life-sized Tardis in their front yard, or add a hot tub in their garage then sit in it watching the hockey game with the garage door open to the alley for all to see. It is a very far cry from the grey, drab and uniform housing in northeast England.

The main shopping street, the west end of 13th Avenue, is lined with boutique shops and independent businesses, and it was on this strip that The Penny University eventually took refuge. Within a few blocks in either direction of the bookstore's second home are a purple-painted parent-and-baby shop (full of slings and cloth diapers and knitted booties and other funky Earth Mother type devices), a live music and events venue, an Irish pub, a neon-green shop selling loose leaf tea, a boho clothing boutique, a fifties-style diner, a yoga studio, a stationery shop, a bright blue ice cream parlour with pink windowsills and green steps, and a "new age" store selling books, crystals and the same patchouli incense sticks that define those shops the world over. Further down, there is a chocolatier, a vegetarian restaurant, and a bakery that bakes cupcakes inspired by the seven deadly sins. If that weren't enough, there is also a craft brewery, six coffee shops crowded into nine blocks, and for some reason, a place selling "fresh Pacific fish" despite the fact that we are 1500 km from the ocean. As I walked back from Safeway one evening, I caught sight of a Disney Princess, carrying two disembodied polystyrene heads in wigs under her arms. This was not the weirdest thing I have seen on my way home. I later discovered that a "Princess Party Store" had opened next to the dentist.

Cathedral is definitely the sort of area where an eclectic, independent bookstore would fit, and in fact, it surprised me that someone hadn't beaten me to it. The building we ended up in after the panicked evacuation from Sylvia's freezing pit of despair had been many other things before the lingerie shop: notably, an ethnic clothing boutique, and a wool and yarn place that held regular knitting classes. Before we officially signed the lease, its most recent tenant had been a temporary constituency office for the local NDP MLA too.

It was somewhat of a surprise then, that the inside of it was deep purple with bright orange feature walls. The NDP tenant may have explained the orange, but they were not there long enough to have undertaken any decorating to my knowledge. Orange and purple do not scream "lingerie" to me. Rather, they just scream. I am a big fan of purple and felt that it was 'meant to be' as soon as I saw it, but even I admit that the contrasting orange was too much for a cosy bookstore effect. Ian, Astrid and I engaged in intense debates over the colour scheme, but I argued that since I was paying for the renovations and the one doing the painting, I got the final decision. I lightened the purple to a pale lilac, toned down the orange to a peachy shade, and eventually had bright, cheerful space reminiscent of our fantastic prairie sunsets. Still colourful and unique, but not headache-inducing.

It was during this difficult and physically demanding renovation period that I learned to love power tools. On top of all the painting, I also got to destroy—I mean, dismantle—four changing rooms in the back of the building that had been used as a space for people to try on bras. Using a Sawzall reciprocating saw and a very large mallet was much more fun than I expected, and I even enjoyed re-plastering the walls. In complete contrast to Sylvia, when I asked permission to take down the changing rooms and repaint the place, our new landlords just shrugged and let me get on with it. It was glorious. The couple that own the building are now our fairytale knights in shining yoga pants, our heroes and saviours from the fearsome dragon, or Old Mortification, or any of the other less printable names we used for Sylvia. Better still, in the new space we have a functional bathroom, a kitchen sink to wash up coffee equipment hygienically, a proper mail slot, and a carpet! The luxury was overwhelming at first. Once we were settled in properly, I installed a bike rack outside, for myself and the random unicyclist.

I don't think we lost any customers in The Great Move; according to my bike computer, it is just 860 metres between the old bookstore and our new Cathedral location. Most of our customers probably lived in Cathedral anyway, and they soon returned to us, admiring the new space. We also began to attract many more local writers. I welcome them all! It has always been part of my bookstore mission to provide a stockist for locally authored books, and we had no shortage of writers wanting to take me up on that offer.

I am very much "at home" in Cathedral, and I'm in great company— which is not a feeling I've experienced in many other places. I embrace the hipster-doofus aesthetic. Having my business somewhere along the 13th Avenue strip was a dream of mine ever since we first moved here, but because there is so much competition for space, it took me nearly a decade to achieve it. Sylvia's building was as close as I could get when I first opened The Penny University. That may have ended abruptly and unpleasantly in a cruel "plot twist" I did not see coming, but it did put us on track to end up exactly where I wanted to be all along.

22
POPES, POETS AND PORTALS

The disembodied head and half-torso of Archbishop Matheiu appearing out of a concrete block on the grounds of the cathedral stares at us through our window, arms outstretched. He looks welcoming, most of the time. "Behold! Books!" he seems to say. Sometimes, someone puts a disposable mask on him, which I appreciate. On quieter days, it's nice to have company, albeit the silent, pious type.

Since the Big Move, I opted to start opening the store on Sundays as well, after seeing substantial crowds of people opposite us in the Cathedral parking lot on Sunday afternoons. In the bookstore, my staff have been asked on multiple occasions if we sell Bibles, or where our Christian section is, and I think those questions arise because of our proximity to the Cathedral. My usual response is to direct people to the "church supply store" further east on 13th Avenue. I would never refuse to stock religious books, I just feel underqualified to curate them.

If customers do want my recommendations for enjoyable Catholic literature, I am always happy to show them a local title that was one of the first books we took on consignment in the bookstore. Excited by the opportunity of having a local stockist, a memoir writer and a fellow Cathedral business owner offered to bring in his own marketing materials to help promote his book. Pleased that he was so prepared and forward-thinking, I almost agreed without asking what exactly the "marketing materials" were. As it happens, it pays to find out these things. The book is about life in 1960s Regina and growing up strictly Catholic. It has an old photograph of a particularly imposing nun on the cover. The author told me, straight-faced, that he had blown up the picture until the nun was seven feet high, and printed it on foam board so that it could stand up as a banner to advertise the book. Now, I would never normally dream of discriminating against Holy Sisters, but I had to make an exception for a 7' cardboard one, especially as she would block the entire doorway to my store. I apologetically made excuses about lack of space, and suggested he placed the nun in his own shop first, just to see how things went. The author pretended to take offence to this and assured me I would be eternally damned for my blasphemy. I have had better Tuesdays.

When we moved to the new location, I allowed myself a petty act of revenge for this damnation, by displaying the nun book right next to a new children's book by another local author. The two authors did not know each other, but had crossed paths before: both had been entered into the same category in the Saskatchewan Book Awards the previous year. The tragicomedy Catholic memoir had lost out on the prize for Best Independently Published Book to a highly colourful kids' book about narwhals. Instead of printing me a giant cardboard narwhal, which I may have welcomed more than the nun anyway, the author of this one just gave me a narwhal stuffie with glittery eyes, that Theia fell instantly in love with. The memoirist was extremely disappointed, both in his loss at the book awards, and at my choice of display. His book did sell out in store within six weeks however, and so the narwhal must have done him some favours.

Re-opening the store in the artsy part of town means that we are much more likely to get local celebrity artists visiting us, out of curiosity. Our first was the former poet laureate of Saskatchewan, whose latest book we had placed prominently at the front of the store. I spied him approaching from the window one Saturday morning. The wonderful thing about the big window is that it is backlit by the store: we can see out, but customers can't see inside clearly. Their view is restricted to the array of tenacious houseplants, the vintage globe and the random books with sun-bleached covers that we leave on the windowsill. We have often seen people peering in, noses—or rather, masks—to the glass, wholly unaware that we can see them doing so.

The poet laureate was no exception. He stood back on the sidewalk, taking in the whole window display, then studied the already-faded cover of a book we'd put there because it was originally quite eye-catching. I was just about to leap up from my seat behind the counter to greet him, when I saw him turn, and instead of heading right towards our door, he climbed the steps to his left, and tried the door to the neighbouring yoga studio. All in-person yoga classes were cancelled because of the pandemic, and so the studio was closed, and more importantly—its door locked.

Eventually, he found the right door, complimented us on the "cosy little store," spent some money, checked to see whether we had his book, and left. I regretted not getting him to sign some copies.

Later that day, Zara, the Yoga instructor and our new landlady, told me that she'd received a phone call asking why the bookstore was closed. The poet has asked, quite upset, why the door was locked when the open sign was on. She tried to explain as best she could that he was outside the yoga studio, and that he could tell because the Yoga logo was printed on the door just above the phone number that he had just called. He was apparently adamant that he was in the right place however and couldn't seem to accept that a yoga instructor did not know the opening hours of a bookstore. Although I had quite plainly seen him go up the steps to their door, he never once acknowledged his mistake, neither to her nor to me.

Ding-jangle-Dang-Dang - KURTHUNK!

We have a bell above the shop door; a traditional little brass one that gets knocked by the door spring mechanism as it is pushed open by eager book lovers. It is not an electronic thing requiring a power supply, and mercifully, it is not a button-operated device that my kids could ring repetitively and drive me to distraction.

For the bell to sound, however, the spring on the door hinge has to hit it, and that spring no longer functions as a spring. The soft-closure it is supposed to facilitate is a distant memory. After the bell's cheerful jangle, you get the kur-thunk of a heavy door slamming behind you. The slam of this door is a source of constant irritation to me, because I feel it spoils the cosy atmosphere of the bookstore that I've tried hard to create. Books are all little doorways in a sense; portals to new worlds within their pages. When the main entrance to this fantastical space sounds so jarring and cumbersome and above all, such an obvious physical barrier, all the magic is lost.

As unhandy as we are, we have been unable to remedy this, and so we put signs on the door:

"Please close the door Gently!" on the inside, and "Take care—door slams!" on the outside. Both are positioned right by the door handle in high contrast monochrome.

A busy-looking woman comes in one morning. She pushes the door, and the bell tinkles pleasantly. Astrid and I brace ourselves. The lady steps in, reaches for the hand sanitiser, and we wince in unison at the all-too-familiar crash that follows.

The woman looks annoyed. "You should really get that door fixed!" she exclaims. Astrid explains quietly that we don't know how, but that we had put signs up to warn people.

"Oh, that won't work, people never read nowadays!" she says. She then proceeds to spend twenty minutes browsing books in our bookshop.

23
LOVE IN A TIME OF CORONA

Writing is a dangerous pleasure. To celebrate an article of mine being published, Rielle once kindly made me a necklace engraved with *Don't make me put you in my novel.* I treasure it and have been careful to warn new friends and acquaintances that hanging around with me comes with the condition that they may well end up as characters in my writings. Fortunately for them, most of these scribblings never see the light of day, let alone a publishing contract. People fascinate me, however, and meeting so many strangers in the bookstore provides a great deal of inspiration. Idly, I let my imagination run riot and invent elaborate backstories for the people who come to visit me.

At times, Astrid indulges me with this process and texts me anonymous, overheard conversations worthy of becoming lines of dialogue. One such discussion interrupted my quiet morning swearing at my payroll software.

I'm currently trying not to listen to two people on a date talk about masturbation. Character 1 is a woman who lived in Toronto but is here now and seems to be some sort of academic. Character 2 is a regular man.

I'm not sure if she meant to imply that academics aren't "regular" people, but given I am a lapsed academic myself, I can't say that she's wrong.

Character 1: *I love these couches. I had a similar set when I was a teenager. It's where I discovered masturbation.*

Character 2: *You masturbated on these couches?*

Character 1: *On ones similar to these, yes. Also, I really like this coffee. But I've had too much today and now I'm anxious.*

Character 2: *Drink water? I hear that's a thing human bodies like.*

Character 1: *What if I'm not human?*

Character 2: *Oh right, you're a masturbation monster.*

I can't think of many careers where you would get interrupted by this type of conversation, so I begged Astrid to continue. She informed me that she'd now learned that both characters were Virgos, which apparently is supposed to explain something.

Character 1: *Where have you touched me the most?*

Character 2: *What do you mean?*

Character 1: *Not physically touched, but mentally.*

Character 2: *Okay, I felt you when you were in your house last night. Like, I could sense that you were alone. And you were doing fine but you were a little sad. And I could tell you were thinking about me. And I really felt you in that moment, without either of us saying a word.*

Character 1: *But I wasn't at my house last night.*

ANNABEL WHAT IS HAPPENING? Now they are playing games. I'm scared.

Astrid wisely decided to go wash coffee cups at this point and so the text messages stopped, but I was left unsatisfied and desperate for more. I have no idea how the rest of their date went, and Astrid has never mentioned seeing them again.

Booksellers and publishers throughout Canada always insist that romance books outsell every other genre consistently, year-round. This is definitely not true in The Penny University. We have a very tiny romance section at the back, mainly because I felt we ought to. Of the few books that have ever sold from there, most were queer romances or written by local authors. I feel this says a lot about our local community of book lovers! I am quite happy to stock romances, but so far, I have never been asked to order any in.

We did hold a few events for authors with romance books, and for the most part they were very well received. I usually advise writers to hold their events on Saturday afternoons, which is consistently the busiest time of the week. This worked well for one writer whose new book, *Canine Cupid*, attracted more local dog lovers than romance readers. I couldn't let her bring her dog into the shop unfortunately, but she did sit in our green armchair surrounded by framed photos of her canine companion to read from her books, much to the delight of our weekend customers.

A much harder 'sell' was Jean Roberta's book launch for *Prairie Gothic*. Jean is a very intense, striking woman with a clever sense of humour, and I knew she was well-known amongst the local writing community. I was excited to have her book launch in the shop and offered her the regular Saturday afternoon timeslot. And then I took a look at the book properly. *Prairie Gothic* is lesbian erotica set in what passed for the gay scene in 1990s small town Saskatchewan. Jean is also a fan of reclaiming the word *dyke* and uses it liberally throughout the book. Suddenly 2:00 p.m. didn't seem like the perfect time for this event. Jean just smiled and promised that she would "skip over the naughty bits" as necessary, and most helpfully, brought her own audience along too and managed to sell out of copies very quickly.

I am not a fan of Valentine's Day in general—in fact, as Carl and I are quite nice to each other all year, we have sometimes agreed to spend February 14th being horrible to each other all day, just to make a change.

Another time, we held a competition to see who could find the other the most tasteless, tacky Valentine's card. I won, because the one I got for Carl came in a red cardboard box instead of an envelope, and lit up and played a beeping, tinny version of "Take my breath away" when it was opened. Carl made a good attempt with a 18 inch high card with a cutesy teddy bear on the outside cover that dropped glitter all over me. It was proof enough, if I needed any, that we are indeed soul mates.

Ian and his wife were still in their 'babymoon' phase and Astrid just likes the Valentine's aesthetic in general, so I was convinced to make a fuss of the day in store. We wrapped dozens of mass market paperbacks in brown paper and added heart-shaped stickers on them, and Astrid took great pleasure in writing terrible, corny pick-up lines on the covers. "You're hotter than the bottom of my laptop!" was a particular favourite amongst writers. The lines in no way related to the books, it was all entirely random. We made a display of them, asking people to go on a "Blind Date with a Book" for $10. It was so successful that we had to promise people it would be back every February.

After the difficult winter and the Great Move, my small team and I finally began to feel the love in our new location. One extremely positive thing to come out of the pandemic was a strong "shop local" movement. At times when we couldn't travel far beyond our city, and when crowded shopping malls were best avoided, I did worry that everyone would just shop online. I did my best to promote our web store and show that, as well as books shipped through Canada Post, we also offered curbside pickups and local deliveries—by bicycle no less. However, I was pleasantly surprised and reassured that people did just drop in to the shop, despite all the restrictions. There is a huge local Facebook group called "I Support Local Business-Regina" and I would go as far as to say that it has saved more than a few local businesses in the past couple of years.

Marketing ourselves as a *local* store also shifted our focus even more on to locally written books and I am proud of how many small events we managed to cram in while adhering to the masking and social distancing policies and capacity restrictions. One prolific children's author brought her six books in, and her four children, and all their friends. It was almost uncomfortably crowded with small, noisy humans, but it was delightful to see them all running about enjoying themselves, and Theia made a lot of new friends that day.

Another favourite author of mine, Mark Allard-Will, is a fellow Brit now settled in Saskatoon. Mark is the author of a graphic novel, all about Vikings, titled *Siegfried: Dragon Slayer*. The book is beautifully illustrated, and painted entirely in coffee, so it obviously appealed to me. For his launch, he not only travelled all the way from Saskatoon for one afternoon, but did so in full Viking costume, complete with leather spats and a fur cloak. He spent a merry afternoon chatting about the influence of Nordic sagas on Tolkien, and his imagined idea of ancient Scandinavia.

I love discovering and meeting such a vast array of interesting characters through the shop. It was a slow and painful process, but throughout 2021, I think the people of Regina gradually began to move beyond *100 Years of Solitude* and towards *Love in a Time of Cholera*. The two novels by Gabriel Garcia Marquez were often cited on social media as "Best books to read in the pandemic"—but mainly for the titles, I assume. *100 Years of Solitude* concerns itself not only with isolation (described as a sort of curse and caused by the Buendias family's inability to fall in love) but with conflicts between traditions and change, and reality and fantasy. In many ways it has parallels with our collective experiences of solitude, paranoias and weird superstitions concerning the pandemic over the last few years. The book's ending is extremely bleak, however, as the family at the centre of the novel never truly overcome their conflicts and there is no hope of redemption for them at the conclusion. Those looking for an uplifting book to inspire hope as we endure the pandemic may be better off with *Love in a Time of*

Cholera—the parallels are more direct. A cholera outbreak provides the background for the beginning of the novel, and when the protagonist, Florentino, is separated from his love, Fermina, he pines for her and the symptoms of his lovesick state are mistaken for symptoms of cholera. While in quarantine, Florentino writes sentimental, immature poetry. His saving grace is not a cure for cholera, or any overtly heroic deed, it is patience, and practice. It takes over fifty years for the pair to reunite, and Florentino finally wins over Fermina *through his writing*.

This feels like a good allegory for my little bookstore. I was initially separated from my lovely customers, and I can't cure Covid-19, but I could patiently wait it out and provide a home for those practising their writing craft and their lovelorn poetry. We were all still at sea, but we know that love awaits us, if we are patient enough.

24
DRIVING TOWARDS A HEALTHY SOCIETY

With all the changes to public health orders in Saskatchewan during the pandemic, it was inevitable that I became embroiled in at least one online argument about the restrictions. The most notable was on the advent of the vaccine mandate, in October 2021. Businesses, city and government facilities, venues and events were required to check for proof of vaccination before allowing people in. Of course, there was uproar, with people claiming that not being allowed access to public spaces placed restrictions on their freedom. I pointed out that this is only reasonable, and akin to having to have a driving licence. This did not go down well.

"I can't believe you're comparing an experimental vaccine to driving a damn car!" someone wrote (without the punctuation.) I do believe it's a fair comparison. 1,745 people died in car crashes in Canada in 2020, 87 of them in Saskatchewan. According to Statistics Canada, of the 81.2 million doses of the Covid-19 vaccines administered in Canada (as of March 2022), "serious" side effects have been reported in 0.010% of cases with zero deaths reported. Meanwhile, Covid-19 has killed 37,027 people. You are more likely to catch Covid-19 than be killed in a car crash, but you are much, much more likely to be killed on the roads than by getting the vaccine.

The majority of people do actively try to prevent dying and killing people with their vehicles. It's a given that you don't go driving on a highway unless you know how to drive a car—and to prove that, you need a driving licence. As I have shown throughout this saga, I do not have a driving licence. I *do* have my Learner's, and I have completed the mandatory basic training—on both sides of the Atlantic no less, and as a result, on both sides of the road too. But I have failed my test numerous times and although I *theoretically* understand how to operate a car, I do not consider myself a safe driver in practice. If I were to drive out on public roads without my licence, even if I thought I could manage it, I'd still pose a risk to others around me. Of course, accidents and collisions still happen even when everyone has their licence, but, and this is the key point, *making licences mandatory for operating a vehicle lessens the risk.*

Crucially, it is my choice, and my decision not to get my licence. I am "living in fear" as the Tweeters would call it, as I am just as nervous about contracting the virus as I am about both my own hopelessness with driving as well as the negligence of other drivers on the road. With that decision comes the consequences: I can't actually leave Regina by myself unless it's by plane, because there are no longer any intercity or interprovincial buses and no passenger trains. I can't see a movie at the drive-through alone nor make my own way to Costco. The lack of bus routes to the outer extremes of Regina does bother me, but given we were supposed to be staying home and avoiding crowds, it has made little difference in the last couple of years. I fully accept the consequences of my decision. It never occurred to me that my rights to access public spaces are being infringed—I can't use public highways because doing so would put *other people* at risk. So, I don't.

The same can be said of Covid-19 vaccines. At the height of the Delta wave of Covid-19, you couldn't go into Saskatchewan restaurants without proof of vaccination, because you could pose a risk to other people if you did. (Even if you think you're healthy, Covid-19 can be asymptomatic.) Of course, sometimes the virus spreads anyway, but vaccination lowers the risk. You can always still choose not to get vaccinated—but you have to make that decision while accepting the consequences of doing so. Having to show proof of your vaccinations is not an infringement on your rights, it's a way of upholding the right to safety of others.

I also tried to fit the idea of masks into this overly extended analogy: I've seen them compared to seatbelts. But this is not truly accurate. Seatbelts protect their wearer; they do little to protect the others in the vehicle. Instead, masks are more like the rear brake lights on a car. They don't make things any brighter for you directly, but other people can see you more easily and avoid running into the back of you. Sadly, the concept of wearing a mask to keep other people safe is what so many internet trolls fail to grasp. To my mind, if you suspect you have Covid-19, refusing to isolate and going out maskless is like driving while drunk. Saskatchewan has one of the highest rates of impaired driving accidents amongst the provinces, and four out of every ten fatal vehicle accidents involve a drunk driver. It is common knowledge that notable members of the Saskatchewan provincial government have DUIs on their records. It seems fitting then, that Scott Moe's government was so quick to lift the mask mandates.

In Saskatchewan, the mask mandate has been brought in, lifted, re-introduced, and lifted again, and we're told that it won't be brought back, ever. In the bookstore, I opted to keep the mandate in place even when we didn't have to. Since the proof of vaccination requirement was also lifted, I decided to do "take-out drinks only" to stop people sitting in the store without their masks while drinking coffee. There are only four of us that work at the bookstore. If any one of us gets sick, the whole business is in trouble. It's a risk, but I'd rather lose a few customers than endanger my staff. Of course, this drew some extremely unpleasant comments online, but I am fairly used to that now.

What did prove to be a pleasant surprise was the amount of in-person support we received for this policy. A "thank you" from so many people who, like me, thought lifting the restrictions came far too soon and wanted to keep up their book habits in relative safety. It was wonderfully reassuring to learn that the vast majority of our customers still care about each other, and like our shop enough to put up with the minor inconvenience of a mask.

There was one woman we met during the highly unpopular first mask mandate for whom I felt truly sorry. Everything about her was sparkly— sparkle ball earrings, glittery gel nails and shimmering eyeshadow. Platinum-blonde hair set in a 1950s-Hollywood style. The cover of her book was also sparkly gold on black. She was most definitely someone who did not look comfortable wearing the plain blue disposable masks—I'd have expected her to arrive in one covered in rhinestones or sequins - but she dutifully put one on before launching into her neat and rehearsed elevator pitch about her book. Her sparkliness was made all the more remarkable by the fact that she had suffered through debilitating postpartum depression, and the book was a self-help guide for others experiencing the same. In it, she urged people passionately not to hide their pain and pretend everything was okay when they needed help. Unfortunately—tragically, at the time— she titled the book: *The Smiling Mask*. We had it on consignment for three months, and never sold a single copy.

I do consider it lucky that we met with so little backlash, but that is not to say everyone has embraced our stance on masks. Earlier on, when people were beginning to think that masking in confined spaces seemed like a good idea, a man called the bookstore to ask our policy on it. I confess, at the time we didn't actually have one, which he seemed relieved about, and came in with his small daughter. He seemed very friendly and chatty and said he'd be back. Then, the public health order came in, and we never saw him again.

Someone else called the store to order a book which seemed to be full of "plan-demic" conspiracy theories. The man seemed to be goading us into trying to find it, since apparently it had been "banned" and was no longer available on Amazon. I think he thought we would refuse to bring it in for him. We did some digging. It turned out to be self-published, and still available to us through one of our distributors. So I dutifully ordered in one copy for him, but warned him it would take a while. I don't think he fully believed that I had found the book as the phone call quickly degenerated into a rant about Amazon's censorship and how *they* won't let the truth be printed. I bit my tongue trying not to prolong the call by pointing out that, as a private company, Amazon can stock and sell whatever it wants, just as I could. As a parent, however, I learned a long time ago to pick my battles, and this one was not worth it.

Eventually, this controversial tome arrived—all 89 pages of it. It may have been earth-shattering in its profundity, but I never bothered opening it. I did call the guy back and he almost seemed annoyed that I had ordered and received the book without difficulty. I want people to read! I don't much care *what* they read, and my bookseller's profit margin remains constant regardless of the subject matter. I did, however, take great pleasure in informing him that he would need to wear a mask in the shop when he came to collect the book. This proved too much for him; he sent a friend with an envelope of cash to the store to pick up the book. Evidently the friend didn't mind the masks so much, though I noticed he didn't bother to read the title of the book either.

During the fall of 2020, Saskatchewan had a provincial election, and a year later, the country had a national one. Both events changed nothing, but both were a way of forgetting about the pandemic for a few days, albeit in an expensive manner. Each time, we trotted out our conscientiously curated "balanced" collection of political books. I know we had the Green Party candidate in the shop, several candidates of the provincial NDP, and the one and only local Liberal party candidate. The Leader of the federal NDP, Jagmeet Singh, did a campaign stop and photo opportunity just outside the bookstore as well. To my knowledge, no Conservative MPs have visited though. I have never met Scott Moe, but I do my best to stock books from across the political spectrum. The soft-spoken Leader of the Opposition (from the provincial NDP) has come to the bookstore often, usually buying books about dragons for his son. I found out later—too late to get them signed—that he has his own book out. It's called *A Healthy Society* and is authored by Dr Ryan Meili. Only in Saskatchewan would the electorate reject an actual medical doctor to lead the province through a pandemic. Truth is even stranger than fiction, and this is why we *need* a bookstore.

25
ON COWBOYS AND GHOSTS

In June, the canola is in full bloom on the prairie. Somehow the sharp yellow on the flatness only serves to make the scenery more alien. Our family has acclimatised to the stark emptiness of the prairies fairly well, but having spent the entire pandemic in the city, the change to country scenery comes as a surprise.

In May 2021, I decided to buy a house in a tiny little town in the middle of nowhere. Kennedy, Saskatchewan is a two-hour drive from Regina. The drive is a long straight line southeast. We pass through a few other Saskatchewan towns en route, but none as small as Kennedy. There's a bison herd that Theia loves to wave at outside Glenavon, and a miniature Eiffel Tower by the edge of the highway at Montmartre. Otherwise, it is two hours of flat farmland occasionally punctuated with grain elevators and the changing colours of the seasons. Carl encourages the kids to count and identify different species of roadkill as we go.

The backstory to this escapade is lengthy and complicated but, suffice to say, suddenly I had money that I wasn't quite sure what to do with. It did *not* come from the bookstore business. With immense gratitude to my late grandmother, I inherited a small fortune unexpectedly, and made the assumption that money invested in real estate is at least as useful as money sitting in the bank earning less than 0.5% interest. Of course, the sensible thing to do would have been to pay down the mortgage on our house in Regina, but that is not how the best adventures begin.

There are many ghost towns in Saskatchewan, places that used to be bustling when the railway ran through them, or when someone struck oil, or before people had migrated towards Saskatoon or Regina. But, inevitably, the railway was rerouted, the oil wells ran dry, or the younger generation gravitated towards larger, more prosperous urban centres. All that's left in many of these towns is the solitary stone church, abandoned buildings lodged at strange angles, deformed by the vicious prairie winds, and a lonely grain elevator. In oil-based ghost towns, the grain elevator is replaced by lonely pump-jacks, colloquially called "nodding donkeys," some of which nod no more. They are an eerie, tragic sight.

For Milo's 12th birthday, instead of a hectic pre-teen party, he opted to spend the day searching out and exploring ghost towns with his Best-Friend-of-the-Moment (I cannot keep up with the ever-changing friendship dynamics). Google maps and Wikipedia searches gave me leads on three ghost towns that were just about "on the way" to Kennedy, so we merrily drove around southern Saskatchewan admiring abandoned barns before ending up in our little project-house for the night. Perhaps the best of the ghost towns was Bromhead, which appears to have been abandoned sometime in the early 1960s. There was still an old gas station, its pump for leaded petrol frozen at 84 cents per gallon. The kids climbed precariously into an old house where the deck had collapsed leaving the front door hanging off one hinge four feet off the ground. Inside, they found a rather disgruntled raccoon that had made a nest in the loose stair carpet. The basement was entirely flooded with water so black and still that at first we didn't notice it was wet and nearly climbed the stairs down into it. As Carl drove into Kennedy that night, I realised we had driven over 300 km and had not seen a single other person since we left Regina. It was definitely the most fascinating of Milo's birthday trips so far.

Kennedy is not quite a ghost town, but if wasn't for the employment created by the huge Loraas recycling plant or the town's proximity to Moose Mountain Provincial Park, it certainly could have been. When the four of us visit Kennedy, the population is boosted to a whopping 220 people! Even so, Kennedy boasts a K-8 school, an ice rink, a post office, a play park, and a library that opens a day and a half a week. The downside is that there is nowhere to get groceries. The nearest Co-op supermarket is an hour's bike ride away in Langbank, and it is closed on Sundays.

Unsurprisingly, the living is cheap out there. We chose Kennedy entirely because we were so shocked by the unbelievably low price of the house. The house we found is technically four bedrooms and is on a triple lot of land. There is no municipal water supply in Kennedy, so the house has a well in the backyard. It froze over the winter and we had to fill water bottles from a public tap outside the tiny town hall. It looks as though the previous owners started renovating the property, but then lost interest or ran out of money, and abandoned the project. The upstairs is renovated, but the downstairs has no walls or proper flooring in two of the rooms. I bought it as a project, thinking it would be fun to do it up, safe in the knowledge that there was little I could do to it that would decrease its value. It could be a great place to go over the summer to get out of Regina. We could even leave my parents and the kids there over the long school holidays while Carl and I stay in the city to work. It was sold off as a foreclosure, and I managed to buy it outright for just $19,000. At that price, why not?

Kennedy is evolving, however, and we soon found that I was not alone in snapping up property for next to nothing. Kennedy now has its own cowboy *cult*. I am not sure cult is exactly fair—it may be more of a commune—but they are certainly a very strange group of people. Their leaders champion a return to a "traditional" way of life; however, you choose to interpret that. Rather ironically, they have a website, and there are more pictures of horses on it than of the people. They bought several of the empty, boarded-up storefronts along the main street of Kennedy with a plan to renovate the whole street with wooden sidewalks and saloon doors and horse posts. So far, they have opened a small General Store (closed over the winter season, unfortunately, but for a brief period we were able to buy bread and milk there without having to drive), a tack shop for horses (obviously a priority), and a diner which was only open for take-out food during the pandemic health restrictions. There is also a homestead being built further out of town. Their literature mentions wanting to start "screen-free" summer camps for kids where they will learn traditional skills and crafts, and horse riding. They are also recruiting a blacksmith, and most interestingly, a doctor. From their Facebook page: *Someone that maybe has been kicked out of their practice for personal beliefs or someone that believes in freedom of choice.* At first glance, that sounded unusually progressive, but I am pretty sure "freedom of choice" here refers to the vaccine mandate, and not a woman's right to choose.

Sending stories and pictures of Kennedy to friends back in the UK results in some interesting reactions. Some of our British friends are unnerved by the lack of horizon, feeling they would get agoraphobic. For others, the concepts of drinking well water and driving 25 km to the nearest grocery shop are unfathomable. To yet others, the cowboys are a source of fascination. But all of them are rendered incredulous by my house purchase.

The colours on the drive out to Kennedy change dramatically from June to July. The canola is flowering making everything unnaturally bright yellow in sharp contrast with the vast blue sky. The pollen makes my eyes itch and induces sneezing fits, and I find the sickly smell nauseating. The heat wave that made the nearby Kenosee Lake soupy and green with algae has also fried our backyard in Kennedy and the grass is now golden straw. The hazy smoke from the northern wildfires drifted down and the sun completely disappeared on our drive home that weekend.

Even the culture is different in rural Saskatchewan. The rural-urban divide is acute and made apparent when looking at election results—but it is more than political. The two-hour drive crosses an intangible cultural border, and so coming out to a new part of the same province in the same country feels more than a little strange to us. Regina is hardly a bustling metropolis, but it is still very different in comparison with Kennedy. I am not really a Big City person, but the quiet open space feels so free to me.

The pandemic has had an enormous effect on the desire to get away and maybe this has influenced my views of Kennedy. I have spent 18 months in one small city with my husband and kids as constant companions. No one has murdered anyone, which I see as a success, but the idea of barricading myself, alone, in the Kennedy house for a few days, unable to take calls from the bookstore and without the kids' videos blaring in the background, sounds *wonderful*. With only the cowboys for company, maybe I shall write a western novel.

I did contact the cowboy organisation to say hello. I have no real intention of joining them, but I did say we would be in the area fairly often. But never for long. I don't think I could stand the Nothingness of the almost ghost town for longer than a few days at a time. I briefly considered whether, when the house is finished, I could rent it out as an obscure lodge for a writing retreat. I quizzed my writing group members about this to see if they would be interested in a prairie getaway. There are certainly no distractions out there, and the mobile phone signal is weak enough to encourage you to unplug from the normal world and have a digital detox. In such a tiny, isolated place, the literary—and movie—trope of small-town secrets and horrors hidden within insular close-knit communities, or maybe evil spirits inhabiting ancient ruined churches, all feel very real indeed. And I'm sure much could be written about the cowboys' antics. But according to members of my writing group, staring out over a featureless prairie dotted only with cows, does not inspire a writer in the same way a cabin in the mountains in British Columbia or a seaside beach hut in the Maritimes would.

Kennedy is crying out for a new coffee row business and I can make a mean "cowboy coffee" (boiling coffee grounds in a pot with no filter), but unfortunately, I cannot see the town being a place that could support a new branch of The Penny University. Nevertheless, despite the less than enthusiastic response from my writing group, Kennedy is so strange to me that it *is* inspirational. After staying in place in the city for so long, a brief trip to the empty wilderness, with a good book to read while I'm there, is a little vacation for us each time I go.

26
THE FAMILIAR STRANGE

In the early 2000s, I took Anthropology as an undergraduate degree. Anthropology is such a large and varied field that it suited someone like me with multiple interests and an inability to make their mind up on a career path. I studied everything from human evolution to the cultural significance of food, to kinship and lineage patterns amongst the Maasai Mara, and ended up writing my dissertation on the colonialist influences on international development projects in education, which is what took me to Nicaragua the first time. I followed this with a master's degree about imagined identities in the online vampire community, and then a Ph.D on the coffee industry. Anthropology covers *everything!*

Unfortunately, before I could get to any of the fun stuff, I had to endure the core theoretical side of the subject, which is seemingly stuck in the 1950s. It's dry, stiff-upper-lipped imperialist social commentary, and it was Margaret Mead who was to be our initial introduction to it all.

In the foreword to Mead's *Coming of Age in Samoa*, Franz Boas described what he saw as the key insight of her research: *The results of her painstaking investigation confirm the suspicion long held by anthropologists that much of what we ascribe to "human nature" is no more than a reaction to the restraints put upon us by our civilization.*

In other words, what is counted as "human nature" is always culturally dependent, and cultural norms are not universal. But at risk of getting too deeply into the interminably philosophical, we also shape our environment. We build cities to inhabit, we tame the wild prairie to have things to eat—but at the same, the environment, the physical geography of a place, shapes our culture as well. As a people, we are heavily influenced by the landscape we reside in, and on a micro-level, our individual psyches are affected by the architecture of our homes, the amount of greenery we can see out of the office window, and in the case of Saskatchewan, how far away the horizon appears. If it appears at all.

This psychogeography is sometimes deliberate and built into the design of a place. It is why people recover quicker in hospital rooms that have windows looking out on to trees and parks, why prisons are always grey and drab, why hipster coffee shops have worn, brown leather sofas and bare brick walls, and why, in my bookstore, it must look like it's always late September and leafy outside. I have lost track of how many people have told me I should get a bookstore cat. These aesthetics are deliberate as they evoke the mood and atmospheres in the spaces that are expected by visitors. Bookstores are always "cosy" and rightly so. It's familiar.

Early anthropological research is severely problematic to the modern reader and couched in the colonial attitudes of the time (read: *casually racist*), but if we can learn everything from Margaret Mead and her work amongst "the primitives"—it is this: to truly understand another place, you must make the familiar seem strange, and make the strange become familiar. Mead, in her hammock in Samoa, did make the tropical island feel familiar after a while, and in doing so, noticed similarities between the Samoan culture and her own.

As many pioneering anthropologists like Margaret Mead eventually came to realise, it is the physical landscape that affects culture, as well as something innate to our human nature. I often think that the British are a cold and unemotional people because there are too many of us crammed into a cold and unchanging environment. We are insular in every sense of the word. There are no extremes of temperature, and fewer sharp contrasts in the seasons to provoke any extreme emotional reactions in the population. Instead, we are the stiff-upper-lipped, "mustn't grumble," Keep-Calm-and-Carry-On sort of folks. There are so many of us on the small island that there is no room for big belly laughs or animated gesticulating, and so the British humour is dry and laconic. Where does that leave Saskatchewanians then? Following this logic, the locals should all be … expansive? Open? Certainly, colourful and vivacious.

It is when pondering things like this that I realise that even after ten years here, despite my adventures, the wonderful friends and arch-nemeses I've made, and the efforts to explore my community through the semi-conscious lens of anthropology, I still have no way of describing the Saskatchewan culture coherently. I am entrenched now, and I am much too familiar to make it "strange" anymore.

A century on from Margaret Mead's adventures, and making the cosy bookstore feel *strange* is one way to examine why we expect it to be cosy in the first place. I have developed a great many habits and routines that aid the day-to-day operations of The Penny University, so much so that I often catch myself walking towards the building as if on autopilot whenever I leave the house, even when I don't need to go in there. There's an exact order to the things I have to do to open the store in the mornings: switch on the lights, boot up the computer, get the coffee machine warming up, turn round the Open signs … and so on. It is all very familiar and repetitive. But every so often, I catch myself looking around the bookstore that I created, thinking, *Where did this come from?* For a split second, it feels very *strange* to be there. That brief blink of strangeness—of unfamiliarity—is useful, as it is an abrupt reality check: my customers are not as familiar with the store as I am, and that many are seeing the place for the first time. The feeling serves as a reminder that the bookstore should not appear *too* strange to the new visitor.

Anthropologists cannot start out from the belief that their own world is "normal." Normal and familiar are relative. People have certain expectations, and businesses succeed when, to a certain degree, they fulfil these expectations. The Penny University does well not in spite of it being eccentric, colourful and more than a little disorganised—but *because* it is that way.

I actively try to achieve the magic of the fictitious "little shop that's always been there but wasn't there yesterday." I attempt to blend the business into the community so it feels to my customers like I have always been here, but still keeping the pleasant surprise when they first discover us. Eventually, I want them to get so acclimatised to our existence that they can't imagine the area without our bookshop. The aim with any business is to make the customer feel comfortable, and they are unlikely to frequent or spend money at places that feel too alien or unfamiliar to them.

I was going to end this book with a celebration of the end of the pandemic, a triumphant return to "normal" and to have the bookstore operating at full capacity with our grins on display and the coffee bar crowded with people. Two years in, and that hasn't happened yet. It may never happen, and I am equally happy with that scenario. We are still masked and cautious, but that is a mere inconvenience and no longer feels apocalyptic. If anything, we have made the pandemic feel "familiar."

We have escaped the mafia's clutches, and avoided the Mad Old Woman In The Attic, we survived the fall of the house of Usher, and endured the still air that bites. Fuelled by coffee and inspired by literature, we've brought the joy and magic of books to Regina, and did it all mainly by bicycle. And so, we soldier on in this weird world, in our friendly, familiar-but-strange neighbourhood, in the city that acts like a small town; a little smudge of grey on the enormous golden prairie. We've found our place with our colourful community of writers, booklovers and doofuses and the thousands of lives we are privy to, between the pages and outside of them.

BOOKS CITED

- Adams, Douglas. *The Hitchhiker's Guide to the Galaxy: A Trilogy in Five Parts*
- Aiken, Joan. *Nightbirds on Nantucket*
- Allard-Will, Mark. *Siegfried: Dragon Slayer*
- Baigent, Michael, et al. *Holy Blood, Holy Grail*
- Bjork, Samuel. *I'm Travelling Alone*
- Bronte, Charlotte. *Jane Eyre*
- Brown, Dan. *The Da Vinci Code*
- Brown, Dan. *Origin*
- Cohen, Leah Hager. *Glass Paper Beans*
- Corey, James S. A. *The Expanse*
- Crace, Jim. *Quarantine*
- Dickens, Charles. *Great Expectations*
- Dickens, Charles. *A Tale of Two Cities*
- Ellis, Markman. *The Coffee-House*
- Ellmann, Lucy. *Ducks, Newburyport*
- Ferguson, Will. *Beauty Tips from Moose Jaw*
- Ferguson, Will and Ian Ferguson. *How to be a Canadian*
- Fitzgerald, Penelope. *The Bookshop*
- Friere, Paulo. *Pedagogy of the Oppressed*
- Gaiman, Neil, and Terry Pratchett. *Good Omens*
- Gaiman, Neil. *American Gods*
- Gane, David, and Angie Counios. *Along Comes a Wolfe*
- Garcia Marquez, Gabriel. *100 Years of Solitude*
- Garcia Marquez, Gabriel. *Love in a Time of Cholera*
- Gibbons, Stella. *Cold Comfort Farm*
- Greer, Andrew Sean. *Less*
- Gregson, Tyler Knott. *Chasers of the Light: Poems from the Typewriter Series*

- Hoeg, Peter. *Miss Smilla's Feeling for Snow*
- Hooper, Emma. *Etta and Otto and Russell and James*
- Joinson, Suzanne. *A Lady Cyclist's Guide to Kashgar*
- Krause, Suzy. *Sorry I Missed You*
- Loblaw, David Robert. *David G Grade 3: The Tragicomic Memoir of a Reluctant Atheist*
- Lohans, Alison. *Canine Cupid*
- Mae, Nicole. *Youth*
- Manson, Mark. *Everything is F*cked: A Book about Hope*
- Mead, Margaret. *Coming of age in Samoa*
- Meili, Ryan. *A Healthy Society*
- Mootoo, Shani. *Polar Vortex*
- Munsch, Robert. *Pyjama Day*
- Munsch, Robert. *50 Below Zero*
- O'Reilly, Carla, et al. *The Smiling Mask: Truths About Postpartum Depression and Parenthood*
- Orwell, George. *Keep the Aspidistra Flying*
- Orwell, George. *1984*
- Pepys, Samuel. *The Diary of Samuel Pepys: The Great Plague of London & The Great Fire of London, 1665-1666*
- Pratchett, Terry. *The Light Fantastic*
- Pratchett, Terry. *Lords and Ladies*
- Rice, Bruce. *The Vivian Poems*
- Rice, Waubgeshig. *Moon of the Crusted Snow*
- Roberta, Jean. *Prairie Gothic: A Tale of the Old Millennium*
- Sax, David. *The Revenge of Analog*
- Schroeder, Andreas. *Dustship Glory*
- Stevens, Kenneth. *2020*
- Stuart, Douglas. *Shuggie Bain*
- Swanson, Cynthia. *The Bookseller*

- Townsend, Annabel. *It Seemed Like a Good Idea at the Time: Ten Years of Misadventures in Coffee*
- Verne, Jules. *Around the World in Eighty Days*
- Viorst, Judith. *Alexander and the terrible, horrible, no good, very bad day*
- Wellborn, Ruth. *Never Rub Noses With a Narwhal: An Alliterative Look At The Arctic*
- Wells, H. G. *The Crystal Egg*
- Wells, H. G. *The Magic Shop*
- Welsh, Irvine. *Trainspotting*
- Wolfe, Beatrice. *Wolf Woman*
- Woolfe, Sue. *Leaning towards infinity: how my mother's apron unfolds into my life*

ABOUT THE AUTHOR

Annabel Townsend completed her first degree in Anthropology, her second in Social Sciences, and her PhD in Human Geography. Her doctoral thesis focused on the concepts of quality in the specialty coffee industry, literally making her a Doctor of Coffee. In 2012, she and her family emigrated to Saskatchewan where she has owned several coffee shops and now her first bookshop-cafe. When not making coffee or selling books, she writes, cycles, and enjoys life on the flat Canadian Prairie.